The New Americans
Recent Immigration and American Society

Edited by
Steven J. Gold and Rubén G. Rumbaut

A Series from LFB Scholarly

Bi-Cultural Competence and Academic Resilience among Immigrants

Rosalva Vega Vargas-Reighley

LFB Scholarly Publishing LLC
New York 2005

※ 5796 5704

Library of Congress Cataloging-in-Publication Data

Vargas-Reighley, Rosalva Vega, 1961-
  Bi-cultural competence and academic resilience among immigrants /
Rosalva Vega Vargas-Reighley.
     p. cm. -- (The new Americans)
  Includes bibliographical references and index.
  ISBN 1-59332-064-7 (alk. paper)
  1. Teenage immigrants--California. 2. Teenagers with social
disabilities--California. 3. Acculturation--California. 4. Academic
achievement--Social aspects--California. 5. Resilience (Personality
trait)--California. 6. Home and school--California. I. Title. II. Series:
New Americans (LFB Scholarly Publishing LLC)
  HV4011.C2V37 2005
  373.794'01'9--dc22

2005004911

ISBN 1-59332-064-7

Printed on acid-free 250-year-life paper.

Manufactured in the United States of America.

Table of Contents

List of Tables and Figures

Tables

Figures

Acknowledgements

This book came about through the generous support of key people. First of all, I would like to thank Dr. Carolyn Aldwin. Dr. Aldwin provided me with invaluable support, guidance, and encouragement throughout the research and writing phases of this manuscript. Secondly, I am indebted to Drs. Keith Barton, Yvette Flores-Ortiz, Patricia Gandara, Barbara Merino, and Adaljiza Sosa-Riddell for their ample support and suggestions during the research phase of this project. Thirdly, I owe a special debt of gratitude to the following UC Davis students for their support in the collection of the data: Jennifer Alvarez, Eliseo Gonzales, Yesenia Huerta, Vanessa Larios, and Nicole Zuniga.

Further, I would like to acknowledge the generous financial support of the Chicana/Latina Research Center of UC Davis and the Jastro Shields Foundation. Also, I would like to thank Christine Brooks for her assistance with the layout and production of the book, and I would like to acknowledge my sister, Angela Sanchez Wimmers. for the final editing of the manuscript. Lastly, I would like to thank Leo Balk from LFB Scholarly for his editorial assistance.

Preface

The relationship between bicultural competence and academic resilience has received ample theoretical support. The empirical evidence regarding this relationship has been inconsistent and inconclusive, however. No studies have systematically examined the relationships among bicultural competence, stress and coping processes across contexts, adaptive processes, and academic resilience.

The present study examined group differences in bicultural competence, stress and coping processes across contexts, self-esteem, depressed mood, academic goals, perceived parental warmth, perceived school discrimination, and academic resilience (i.e., GPA). Further, within-group associations among these factors also were assessed. Lastly, a number of structural equation models also were explored herein to determine which model offered a stronger explanation of the factors related to academic resilience.

Participants were Latina/o (n = 103) and Southeast Asian (n = 89) 9th-grade youth from two high schools in Northern and Central California. An additional 78 Latina/o 9th-grade youth from a Northern California rural middle school participated in only the factor analyses.

Results of the between-group analyses indicated that the Latina/o group was more likely to experience greater stress in the familial situation, including greater parental/marital dysfunction, more severe stressors, and greater stress ratings. The Southeast Asian group was more likely to be an immigrant sample with lower socioeconomic status (SES), but was more likely to reveal greater grade advancement, higher GPA and academic goals.

Results of the within-group analyses and the structural equation analyses indicated that bicultural competence was related to greater self-esteem, social support coping and coping efficacy in the familial stressful situation, direct action coping and coping efficacy in the academic stressful situation. Further, coping efficacy across contexts was associated with greater self-esteem, which I turn was related to higher GPA. The analyses revealed that there was a marginal indirect relationship between bicultural competence and GPA via self-esteem.

In the environmental factors and outcomes exploratory model, perceived school discrimination was related to lower self-esteem, which in turn, was related to lower GPA. The analyses revealed that there was a significant indirect relationship between perceived school discrimination and GPA via self-esteem.

Improved understanding of the relationships among these factors may have important implications for designing dropout prevention and intervention programs for educationally at-risk ethnic youth.

CHAPTER 1

The Relationship of Academic Resilience and Bicultural Competence

INTRODUCTION

> Children do not grow up in a vacuum. They cannot be understood apart from the historical, geographical, and socioeconomic characteristics of the area in which they develop. As evaluators, we are reminded, ever and again, that the children we see are members not only of families but also of wider groups, whose training patterns affect them a good deal. To do our work well, we need to be aware of these cultural patterns; only then will we be able to understand the child's own functioning and that of his family in an adequate way.
>
> -Looff (1979, pp. 87-88)

Early adolescence has been conceptualized as both a period of discontinuity as well as a period of continuity (see Lerner et al., 1996). Adolescents are believed to undergo major systemic changes in the biological, psychological, and sociocultural realms (e.g., puberty and identity). Despite these changes, some aspects of cognition, behavior, and personality remain continuous from childhood through adolescence, such as core values (see Lerner et al., 1996). Youth differ, however, in their ability to integrate changes. Some youth appear to maneuver these transitions relatively unscathed while others appear to falter. How do we understand these differences in negotiating the challenges which adolescence may entail to some youth?

In Werner and Smith's (1982) longitudinal study of a developmentally at-risk cohort of children from the island of Kawaii, one-third of their sample did not succumb to a negative outcome, but rather, they thrived. Similarly, other studies find that a number of resilience factors, both internal (e.g., biculturalism) and external (e.g., social support), may attenuate the impact of an at-risk status (see Portes & Rumbaut, 2001; Suárez-Orozco & Suárez-Orozco, 2001).

From a developmental contextual perspective, individuals are seen to differ as well as in their sociocultural contexts. Lerner et al. state that constraints on change may arise from both the organism and the context. These authors endorse a transactional framework to study developmental change in adolescence. From this perspective, the organism as much shapes the context as the context shapes the organism, and that at the same time, both organism and context constrain the other. For example, an avoidantly-insecurely attached child may solicit behaviors from a caregiver that are consonant with her or his attachment style. In this instance, the child may consistently ignore or reject the caregiver's overtures for physical contact. The caregiver may feel thwarted in her or his attempts to physically connect with the child, which may lead to a gradual extinction of the behavior. In this way, the caregiver's behavior towards the child in turn may reinforce the child's attachment style. Unfortunately, such a scenario not only reinforces the child's attachment style, but it also impinges on her or his opportunity to develop a secure attachment. In this manner, the individual constrains her or his environment as well as the environment constrains the individual.

Development is understood by these authors as a transactional or dynamic process between an organism and her or his environment. Lerner et al.'s model points to the complexity inherent in understanding developmental change or discontinuity. Their model underscores the importance that the individual or group needs to be understood within context.

Lerner et al. believe that because of the profound character of the changes across the early adolescent period, this time of life, more so than any other developmental transition, represents a period of potential risk as well as a period of potential resiliency. Most youth find individual resources and contextual supports to cope and adjust adequately to the stressors inherent in adolescence; but early adolescence also is seen as a period where alarmingly increasing numbers of youth do not cope or adjust successfully. Behaviors such as suicide, drug use, violent crime, teenage pregnancy (Dryfoos, 1990), HIV infection, chronic unemployment, and dropping out of school (Ianni & Orr, 1996) may be consequences of inadequate coping and adjustment during this developmental period.

Each of these problems can have negative effects on individual development, family and societal functioning. Researchers note that these problems and their sequelae are often interconnected, combining and reinforcing each other with devastating effects for youth, their communities, and society at large (Ianni & Orr, 1996). Dropping out of school may lack the intensity of some of these other problems of youth; nevertheless, it may be viewed as a significant crisis on multiple levels. For one, early school exit is believed to be directly associated with youth unemployment (Ianni & Orr, 1996) and results in increased concentration of youth in low-wage, unstable work, and contributes to disproportionately high rates of individual and family poverty, which may have long-term social and economic consequences on the development and stability of the U.S. economy (Darder, Torres, & Gutierrez, 1997).

Much is known about the factors that predict academic failure and attrition or early school exit, but not as much is known about the factors that predict academic resilience, especially in ethnic youth. Risk factors such as poverty, discrimination, and familial mental illness may be instrumental in helping us to identify which populations are in need of services, for example, but they tell us very little about what factors promote academic resilience in these populations. Further, this information tells us very little about individual differences, or why it is that some ethnic educationally at-risk youth do not dropout prematurely, but rather, excel academically.

Therefore, the proposed study takes a strength as opposed to a deficit model perspective. By understanding what factors promote resilience it is argued that we may be more effective at designing prevention and intervention programs that build on existing strengths. Academic protective factors include family and peer support, individual persistence, a sense of belonging to school, a supportive academic environment, value placed on school, participation in extracurricular activities, and placement in a college preparatory track (Gonzalez & Padilla, 1997). However, very little is understood on how bicultural competence and coping processes beyond social support affect academic performance in ethnic youth.

In the current investigation, the acculturation framework was used to examine how bicultural competence may relate to academic resilience. Bicultural competence refers to the ability to develop and maintain competence in two cultures (see LaFromboise, Coleman, & Gerton, 1993). Academic resilience refers to the ability to sustain high levels of achievement motivation and performance despite an at-risk status (see Gonzalez & Padilla, 1997). In addition, the coping process framework was employed to examine how stress and coping processes across contexts also may relate to academic outcome. Thus, this study provided a link between two different literatures (the acculturation literature and the stress, coping, and contextual processes literature), a major goal of this project.

A second aim of this study was to examine the connections among bicultural competence, stress, coping, and contextual processes, and academic resilience in academically at-risk ethnic youth (i.e., Latina/o and Southeast Asian adolescents). While some researchers have gathered information about both bicultural competence and coping among specific ethnic groups (see LaFromboise, Coleman, & Gerton, 1993), they did not examine the relationship between these factors systematically or cross-culturally. An investigation of the relationship between bicultural competence, stress, and coping processes across contexts, and academic resilience cross-culturally may provide insight regarding the reasons why there are both individual and ethnic differences in academic outcomes. Further, a number of exploratory factors were investigated herein to determine their relationships with the aforementioned variables. These are discussed further in Chapter 5.

The primary hypotheses of this study addressed ethnic group differences in bicultural competence, stress and coping processes across contexts, academic resilience, and the exploratory variables of self-esteem, depressed mood, academic goals, perceived parental warmth, and perceived school discrimination. The secondary hypotheses examined within-group associations among these three types of factors and sought to explore whether bicultural competence is directly or indirectly related to academic resilience via stress and coping processes across contexts. Further, alternative study and exploratory structural equation models also were explored herein.

Specifically, this study explored whether bicultural competence is directly or indirectly related to academic resilience via lower stress ratings across the familial and academic contexts, greater likelihood of appraising stress as challenges across contexts, greater problem-focused coping in the academic context, greater social support coping in the familial context, and greater coping efficacy across contexts. The exploratory variables of self-esteem and depressed mood also were incorporated into this model as outcome or dependent variables along with academic resilience (see Chapter 5). Lastly, alternative study and exploratory models were offered to determine whether these models provided a better explanation of academic resilience than the original study model (see below).

The next three chapters (Chapters 2, 3, and 4) survey the academic performance, bicultural competence, and stress and coping processes within context literatures. In Chapter 5, a cross-cultural model for the relationships among bicultural competence, stress and coping processes across contexts, exploratory adaptive processes, and academic resilience in Latina/o and Southeast Asian youth is proposed, and alternative study and exploratory models are introduced. Chapter 6 provides a description of the methods implemented in the study, and is followed by the presentation of the data analyses in Chapter 7. Finally, Chapter 8 discusses the findings, limitations, future directions, and implications of this study.

CHAPTER 2

The Value of Academic Resilience

ACADEMIC PERFORMANCE

> We are not asking our children to do their own best but to be *the* best. Education is in danger of becoming a religion based on fear; its doctrine is to compete. The majority of our children are being led to believe that they are doomed to failure in a world which has room only for those at the top.
>
> -LeShan (1997, p. 18)

> You've seen a herd of goats going down to the water. The lame and dreamy goat brings up the rear. There are worried faces about that one, but now they're laughing, because look, as they return, that goat is leading! There are many different kinds of knowing. The lame goat's kind is a branch that traces back to the roots of Presence. Learn from the lame goat, and lead the herd home.
>
> -Rumi (Barks, 1995, p. 144)

Latina/o Dropout Rates

The number of Americans of Latina/o descent rose from just under 7 million persons in 1960 to approximately 10.5 million in 1970, 14.6 million in 1980, and an estimated 20 million in 1990 (Gutierrez, 1995). The number of ethnic Mexicans, who historically have constituted the largest subpopulation of Latinas/os and who now represent approximately 60 percent of the total, has grown at a similar rate (Gutierrez, 1995). Between 1980 and 1990, the Mexican-origin population increased by 54 percent (Baker, 1996). Hispanics in general are expected to become the largest "minority" in the United States early in the twenty-first century (Perez & Salazar, 1997).

Latina/o refers to persons who live in the United States and who can trace their ancestry back to Latin American countries (De Anda, 1996). Chicanas/os are a Latina/o subgroup and are considered by some to be a population of Mexican descent born in the United States, although currently there is no consensus as to the correct definition of the term Chicana/o (De Anda, 1996).

Hispanics in general are a young population with a median age of 26, which is 7 years younger than that of non-Hispanics (see Chapa & Valencia, 1993). Nearly one-third of the population of Mexican origin is younger than 15, compared with less than one-fifth of the non-Mexican origin population. Further, Latina/o children are the fastest growing ethnic group in public schools (Smith, 1995). Latina/o enrollment in elementary and secondary public schools has doubled over the last two decades from less than 6 percent in 1973 to nearly 12 percent in 1993 (Smith, 1995).

Despite this increase, Latinas/os are significantly under-represented in secondary and post-secondary educational attainment (Lango, 1995). They have been found to be grossly under-represented in higher education (Lango, 1995), over-represented in lower paying jobs (Avalos, 1996), and to have a greater likelihood of living in poverty as compared to Anglos (Smith, 1995).

Significant gender and ethnic differences within this group are evident in the literature. Latina women, particularly Mexican Americans, appear to fare worse educationally and economically. Perez and Salazar (1997) state that "in 1990, almost one-quarter of Hispanic families were female-headed and these families were especially likely to be poor; children who grow up in female-headed families often face high poverty, myriad social problems, and few educational or other opportunities" (p. 71). Some studies report that Mexican American women report the lowest educational attainment rates, the highest levels of unemployment, and the highest poverty levels of any ethnic or gender group in the U.S. (see Vasquez, 1994).

Another significant socio-demographic trend is the differential rates in academic completion amongst rural and urban Latinas/os. Several studies have reported that rural Latinas/os trail both urban Latinas/os and Whites in high school and college completion, as well as functional literacy (see Fratoe, 1981; Rochin & Castillo, 1993).

According to the National Center for Education Statistics (1994), a dropout is defined as "a student who has enrolled during the prior school year, has not re-enrolled at the start of the current school year, has not graduated from high school or enrolled in another state- or district-approved program, has not enrolled in another school district or state-approved program, is not absent for illness or suspension, and is not dead' (cited in Ianni & Orr, 1996, p. 289). According to Ianni and Orr, relatively few students formally withdraw from school, most leave school through a gradual process indicated by infrequent attendance, frequent suspensions and expulsions.

It is commonly known that the dropout rate is high for Hispanics. The National Education Longitudinal Study (NELS), begun in 1988, reported dropout rates between the 8th and 12th grades of 5.1 percent for Asians/Pacific Islanders, 5.7 percent for White, non-Hispanic, 8.4 percent for Black, non-Hispanic, 14.3 percent for Hispanics, and 16.9 percent for Native Americans in the August 1994 assessment phase, while Ianni and Orr (1996) report dropout rates of 29 percent for Hispanic youth, 14 percent for African American youth, and 8 percent for White youth. Furthermore, a report by the National Education Goals (1991) reported that between 1975 and 1990, high school completion rates improved 12% for Black students and 2% for White students, but decreased by 3% for Hispanic students (cited in Perez & Salazar, 1997).

Thus, if one considers the more conservative report, the dropout rate is almost three times higher for Hispanics as compared to Asian or White youth, and is second only to Native Americans who also experience a similarly high dropout rate. Further, high school completion rates for Hispanics appeared to be decreasing. However, these reports may be misleading, because the various Hispanic groups are presumably aggregated; thus, it is not known for certain whether these rates hold for all Hispanic sub-cultural groups. On the other hand, a study which investigated educational attainment levels in the various Hispanic sub-cultural groups found that Mexican Americans had the lowest levels while the "Other Hispanic" group had the highest level of educational attainment of any subgroup (see Chapa & Valencia, 1993).

Southeast Asian Dropout Rates

Asian Americans comprise a diverse range of distinct nationalities, languages, and cultures. Some are recent immigrants or refugees while others are well established in the U.S. As a group, this population has grown from 3.7 million in 1980 to 7.3 million in 1990, which is equivalent to a 95 percent growth within one decade (Ong & Hee, 1993). This rapid growth has been fueled by a continuing flow of immigrants from more than ten different countries (Reimers, 1985).

The latest subgroup of Asian Americans in the United States are the Southeast Asian refugees, a diverse group comprising people from Cambodia, Laos, and Vietnam, who arrived in three different waves since 1975 (Pho, 1994). Vietnamese compose 63 percent of the entering total, while Laotians and Cambodians compose 19 and 17 percent, respectively, of the entering total (U.S. Department of Health and Human Services, 1987). The growth rate of the Vietnamese subgroup alone reached a high of 150 percent between 1980 and 1990 (U.S. Bureau of the Census, 1995).

The age and sex composition of this group reveals that this population on the whole is relatively young – the median age is 25 years, and weighted slightly greater towards the male end (55 percent male vs. 45 percent female) (Huang, 1998). Further, most Southeast Asians are concentrated in the West, with the greatest concentration found in California.

Each wave of the Southeast Asian refugees is distinctive in socioeconomic status, ethnicity, and culture; however, as refugees they share the common experience of exodus from their homes and insertion into an alien country (for a thorough discussion of the characteristics of each wave, see Huang, 1998). Huang notes that mixed emotions such as fear, anticipation, joy, and loss are commonly felt by refugees in such a situation. Furthermore, Huang notes that refugees are subjected to severe stress (e.g., lack of food and medical services) and problems of adjustment (e.g., "culture shock") en-route and in their host's country. Their labor-force participation is lower and their unemployment rate is higher than in the general population (Huang, 1998). Huang notes that in 1990, socio-demographic data indicated that Southeast Asians remain among the most economically stressed and impoverished populations in the United States. Other strains include acculturation and disruption in the family system and roles, in addition to numerous psychological and social problems (see Matsuoka, 1991).

Dropout rates for the Southeast Asian population are difficult to disentangle because all Asian subgroups tend to be aggregated in educational statistical analyses (see Pho, 1994). For example, the National Center for Education Statistics (1992) indicated that there were a substantial number of underachieving Asian eighth graders. Southeast Asian students compromised the third largest group in this sample; however, specific educational rates were not reported for each subgroup. Therefore, it is not known for certain which subgroup(s) are underachieving.

A recent report by the National Center for Education Statistics of the dropout rates in the United States in 1995 similarly aggregated this group into the rather broad race-ethnic category of Asian/Pacific Islander and found a 5.1 percent dropout rate for this group between the 8th to 12th grades in August of 1994, which is the lowest rate across the ethnic groups surveyed. Unfortunately, the ethnic breakdown of this category was not reported in this lengthy, 133-page report; therefore the specific contribution of the Southeast Asian subgroup to this statistic is unknown.

There is some evidence that suggests that there is great variability within the Asian/Pacific Island category. In terms of educational attainment, Sue and Okazaki (1990) report that 82 percent of Japanese complete high school as compared to 61 percent of Samoans. More startling are the dropout rates among the various subgroups. For example, during the 1986-1987 school year, the U.S. Commission on Civil Rights (1992) reported dropout rates of 46.1 percent for Filipino students in California and more than 50 percent for Laotian (i.e., Southeast Asian) students in Lowell, Massachusetts. The limited information available on this group appears to suggest that this population also is at-risk academically.

In sum, these socio-demographic patterns across these distinct cultural groups are noteworthy given that socioeconomic status has been found in the literature to be linked to educational outcome. Ianni and Orr (1996) note that poverty has been identified in the literature as a contributory factor in the dropout phenomenon. Studies find that socioeconomic status (SES) and other aspects of family background are those factors most consistently linked to dropping out (Perez & Salazar, 1997). According to the literature, SES indirectly influences dropout behavior through its influence on other measures of student achievement, such as grades, test scores, and retention (see Rumberger, 1991).

However, socioeconomic status is just one factor that has been linked in the literature to the dropout phenomenon. There are multitudes of other factors that have been identified as contributing to this outcome as well. Further, it is important to point out that not all impoverished individuals or groups drop out prematurely from high school, such as immigrant youths. Some socially and economically disadvantaged individuals and groups continue to view education as a significant means of upward mobility (see Smith, 1995).

Immigration status is also a significant socio-demographic trend in the differential rates of academic completion in Latinas/os. In Rumbaut's (2000) large-scale longitudinal study of 2,420 8th and 9th grade students in schools of the San Diego Unified School District, only 8.7% of Hispanic youth from immigrant families were officially determined to have dropped out of school as compared to 9.7% of Indochinese youths, 10.5% of non-Hispanic White youths, 12.2% of Filipino youths, 17.8% of Black youths, and 26.5% of total Hispanic youths. The Hispanic immigrant youth statistic was second only to the Asian dropout rate at 5.8%. According to this study, immigrant status is related to greater academic completion, not just for Hispanic youth but also for Asian, Filipino, and Indochinese youths.

Rumbaut also found differences amongst Asians in general, Filipinos, and Indochinese. Asians in general had the lowest dropout rate at 5.8% while Filipinos had the highest rate at 12.2%. Whereas Vietnamese youths revealed an average dropout rate (5.5%) and Cambodian (4.3%), Laotian and Hmong youth revealed the lowest dropout rates as compared to other nationalities in the sample (3.9% and 3.8%, respectively). As previously noted, youth from immigrant families revealed lower dropout rates than youth from non-immigrant families (4.5% vs. 5.8% Asians, 4.0% vs. 12.2% Filipinos, and 4.8% vs. 9.7% Indochinese), confirming the protective role of immigrant status.

However, immigrant status does not appear to be related to premature school exit, as evident in Rumbaut's study. Children of immigrants are also plagued by poverty (see Suárez-Orozco & Suárez-Orozco, 2001). Nevertheless, SES has a significant negative impact on school completion by indirectly influencing dropout behavior through its influence on other measures of student achievement such as grades, test scores, and retention (see Rumberger, 1991).

THEORETICAL FRAMEWORKS OF THE DROPOUT PHENOMENON

It is estimated that there are 39.7 million individuals 18 years of age or older nationwide who never completed high school (National Center for Education Statistics, 1993). Particular subgroups of youth appear to be more at-risk of dropping out of high school as noted above. Further, young adolescents between 8th and 10th grades appear to be at greater risk of dropping out. In a longitudinal study of 8th-graders by the National Center for Education Statistics (1994), survey results showed that 12 percent of the cohort dropped out by the time they should have been in the 12th grade, with about half leaving between the 8th and 10th grades (Ianni & Orr, 1996).

A number of assumptions underlie the phenomenon of dropping out of school. For one, dropping out prior to high school graduation is believed to be directly associated with youth unemployment and poverty, and to be indirectly related to a whole host of social and individual ills, such as deviancy (see Ianni & Orr, 1996). Dropping out of school may be viewed as a continuing crisis for youth, their communities (e.g., crime), and society at large (e.g., dependency on welfare). Clearly, this phenomenon does not appear to be advantageous on an individual nor on a societal level.

Explanations for dropping out have focused on the following areas: (1) adolescent development within an institutional context which encompasses both psychological development and social identification theory, (2) social role behavior which encompasses both consumer behavior and role conflict theory, (3) culture conflict which encompasses both adolescents' cultural conflict and institutional culture conflict, and (4) structural domains, which encompasses both the school and interagency structures (Ianni & Orr, 1996).

Some theories and research on the dropout phenomenon have focused on the formation of the self and how the school environment may either promote or thwart healthy identity development. The first major construct of the dropout phenomenon, adolescent development theory, focuses on identity formation and how the sociocultural context impacts this process. From this perspective, the development of self-identities is based on some form of reciprocity between the self-concept and the social structure (see Kohut, 1971; Turner, 1968). The theory argues that how a student is viewed by peers and adult caretakers in her or his educational life is of considerable importance as to how he or she comes to identify the self as a successful learner (Ianni & Orr, 1996). Personal competence, capability, and efficacy are components of a positive self-image from this perspective.

Dropping out, in this view, centers on the developing identity of the individual dropout and the paucity of stimulation for and integration of personal efficacy and self-esteem, allowing for self-identification as a learner (Ianni & Orr, 1996). School failure is viewed as just one link in a long line of further difficulties, failures, and frustrations. A vicious cycle is believed to ensue. For instance, academic failure may contribute to self-identification as a non-learner, which may be reinforced and exacerbated by parental, peer, and teacher interactions; and this may lead to self-perpetuating attitudes and behaviors, such as self-doubt, declining success, and ultimately school withdrawal. Consequently, youth may become involved in alternative, less socially-sanctioned activities as a means by which they may experience some success, thereby recovering some self-esteem (see Ianni & Orr, 1996).

The social identification perspective focuses on how students are involved in school, both on an emotional and behavioral level. From this perspective, successful school completers have multiple, expanding forms of participation in school-relevant activities, such as in club membership (Ianni & Orr, 1996). According to these researchers, students who do not participate in school activities may not develop a sense of identification with school that may lead to significant negative consequences, such as school failure and withdrawal.

The second major perspective on the dropout phenomenon is social role theory. This perspective focuses on the dimension of social roles as it relates to the causes of school withdrawal. Consumer behavior and role conflict are two dimensions within this perspective. Consumer behavior refers to the active process of choice in remaining a student or dropping out; whereas role conflict refers to the stresses that some students experience from the demands of multiple roles (Ianni & Orr, 1996).

From the perspective of consumer behavior theory, a student may be viewed as exercising appropriate consumer behavior by dropping out of school if the school is perceived as not meeting her or his needs due to poor teaching, uncaring attitudes, lack of a culturally relevant curriculum, or a poor physical and social climate for learning (Ianni & Orr, 1996). Ianni and Orr note that oftentimes youth who drop out do not have viable alternatives; poor employment and career prospects, especially for inner-city minority youth, project bleak futures for many. Data from the 1986 Educational Testing Service reported that most Hispanics cited loss of interest in school or boredom, personal reasons, or the need to work as causes for dropping out (cited in Kirsch & Jungeblut, 1986).

However, from the perspective of role conflict theory, dropping out may be seen as a function of role overload or having to juggle too many responsibilities with inadequate time and experiential resources (Ianni & Orr, 1996). Working long hours or having significant responsibilities at home (e.g., childcare) without the value of education, may devalue the role of a student to the point where dropping out is seen as a more viable alternative (see Ianni, 1989). In the literature, marriage, pregnancy, and work are factors that have been suggested as contributors to dropping out (see Perez & Salazar, 1997). Also, competitive or antagonistic peer group and school roles may indirectly devalue the role of student (see Ianni & Orr, 1996). For example, for some peer groups, school success may not be seen as "cool" while deviancy, on the other hand, may be seen as the norm and may even be encouraged.

Culture conflict also has been endorsed as a causal factor of dropping out. This theory focuses on cultural values and the compatibility or incompatibility of diverse sociocultural contexts. From this perspective, the dropout phenomenon is viewed as a cultural problem rather than a consequence of individual differences and circumstances (see Ianni & Orr, 1996). This view approaches the problem from both the students' and the schools' perspectives. From the adolescents' position, dropping out is seen as the result of cultural dissonance or conflict between the school and the community of the adolescent (Ianni & Orr, 1996).

A study by Calabrese and Poe (1990) lends support for this theory. In their sample of 1,064 Midwestern secondary urban school students in grades 7th through 12th, African American and Latino students reported experiencing higher levels of alienation, powerlessness, and isolation than Caucasian students. These experiences in turn are believed to contribute to higher dropout rates (see Calabrese & Poe, 1990; Kulka, Kahle, & Klingel, 1982). The researchers suggest that the socio-cultural context of the school may be perceived as extremely stressful and culturally dissonant for some ethnic youth, thereby contributing to academic failure.

From the schools' position, Ianni and Orr note that "the school formally or informally uses social, racial, and ethnic identification to sort students access to educational resources and reinforces culturally biased perspectives and expectations, it can confuse and sometimes confound the consolidation of an authentic identity as a learner, for it is more discriminated against students" (p. 300).

Fordham and Ogbu (1986) elaborate on this phenomenon in their discussion of the double bind that some African-American students encounter across the contexts of school and the community. They argue that some students do not succeed academically because they are caught in the bind between a school system that refuses to acknowledge their academic achievement and a community that considers academic achievement as "acting White" (Ianni & Orr, 1996).

Further, institutional cultural conflict refers to the professional culture of a school, composed of teachers, school staff and administrators and, more broadly, to the school community. Some argue that the school culture may be dissonant for some students, undermining the sense of community and inclusiveness for these students and discouraging their continued school attendance as well as compromising their school performance (Ianni & Orr, 1996).

Tracking is an example of this phenomenon. Perez and Salazar (1997) note that even within "integrated" or desegregated schools, Latina/o students may be segregated by classroom assignment patterns, such as placement in special education or in sheltered English immersion classes (also see Donato, Mechaca, & Valencia, 1991; Orum, 1986; Valencia, 1991; Valencia & Aburto, 1991). Perez and Salazar also note that Latinas/os tend to be disproportionately enrolled in educational tracks that do not prepare them for either college or stable employment (also see National Council of La Raza, 1992). They argue that this type of non-academic tracking is believed to lead to poor educational opportunity for Latinas/os and other minority students as well.

Another problem that may be classified under the rubric of school culture is enrollment below modal grade level. Perez and Salazar (1997) also note that Latina/o students are more likely than non-Hispanics to be held back in school and enrolled below modal grade level, which according to research is the greatest predictor of later dropping out of school (also see Orum, 1986).

Another example of institutional culture conflict may be gleaned from Kao and Tienda's (1998) focus group study. They found that Black and Hispanic youth of their study were relatively uninformed about college, which they argued impedes their chances of reaching their educational goals. This lack of information is believed by these researchers to contribute to feelings of ambivalence toward academic performance (e.g., not worrying about grades), which ultimately may impact educational achievement. Unfortunately, Kao and Tienda did not discuss why these students lacked information about college. It is plausible that the school context may not be preparing some ethnic youth for college, but it may be equally likely that the familial context also is not preparing students for an advanced education (e.g., lack of role models).

Finally, there are few minority teachers who can act as role models for Latinas/os, Southeast Asians, and other ethnic youth. Studies suggest that because of the limited educational backgrounds of parents and the lack of positive role models for some ethnic youths in their communities, teachers and school administrators may play an even greater role in the educational trajectories of such youth (Perez & Salazar, 1997). Unfortunately, studies point to the deficiency inherent in this domain. For example, studies find that Latina/o students receive less career placement assistance than their peers (see De La Rosa & Maw, 1990).

Some studies point out that the familial context may be dissonant for academic achievement for some youth. Steinberg, Dornbusch, and Brown (1992) argue that Hispanic and Asian American households are typically not conducive to success in school. They argue that authoritarian parenting is relatively higher in these households than the prevalence of authoritative parenting. They add that "in a school system that emphasizes autonomy and self-direction authoritarian parenting, with its emphasis on obedience and conformity and its adverse effects on self-reliance and self-confidence, may place youngsters at a disadvantage" (p. 728). However, Asian American youth are believed to benefit from peer support for academic achievement, which is seen to off-set the negative influence of authoritarianism, whereas Hispanic youth lack this support (Steinberg, Dornbusch, & Brown, 1992). This argument is rather controversial because elsewhere Hispanics have been found to be collectivistic, receiving support from both family and friends with tangible benefits (see Marin & Marin Van Oss, 1991).

Respect for student diversity and the fostering of achievement irregardless of race, ethnicity, gender, socioeconomic status, and ability have been noted in the literature as key criteria necessary for teachers and schools to be successful with all students, especially those at risk of dropping out. Further, studies suggest that an increase in minority school staff would have a positive effect on ethnic youth (see Perez & Salazar, 1997). Lastly, familial and peer support also may have a positive effect on ethnic youths' achievement.

Structural domains theory focuses on society's role in the dropout problem. This perspective shifts in focus from just dropouts to school reform. According to Ianni and Orr (1996), "this perspective includes whether schools can be held accountable for a broad range of social problems that interfere with students' successful schooling, such as the ramifications of poverty and deprivation, the inadequacy of other social institutions, and dramatically increasing social problems such as drug abuse and homelessness" (p. 302).

Perez and Salazar (1997) note that Hispanics are two-and-one-half times as likely as non-Hispanics to live in poverty and to live in neighborhoods with limited opportunities and few resources. These authors note that their schools are likely to have very limited resources as well. Schools in impoverished areas are typically overcrowded, segregated due to "White Flight", under-funded because of a limited tax base, and suffer from a deteriorating infrastructure (see Chapa & Valencia, 1993; Reyes & Valencia, 1993). Further, some homes of youth may lack resources such as books and an appropriate place to study, especially if they are living in crowded and economically poor conditions (Perez & Salazar, 1997). Lack of resources across contexts has been found in the literature to be linked to dropping out of school (see Perez & Salazar, 1997).

Moreover, researchers have shown that impoverished youth are more likely than their more advantaged peers to do poorly in school and to be vulnerable to school failure, teenage pregnancy, and other social problems (see Children's Defense Fund, 1991; Perez & Duany,1992). These social implications may also apply to Southeast Asian youth that are similarly socio-economically disadvantaged, as noted above.

From the structural domains perspective, school reform would focus on intervention and change to existing school system structure and to interagency structures or the links between schools, families, and communities. For example, schools may be held accountable for providing enriching or remedial programs (e.g., prevention and intervention) for disadvantaged youth and their families, such as providing low- or no-cost, extended, high-quality, on-site, after-school, daycare facilities. Such a resource may conceivably decrease the economic stress on families already economically burdened and may provide participating students with access to tutorial services.

In sum, four major theoretical constructs were discussed to understand the dropout phenomenon; these were identity development, social role behavior, cultural conflict, and structural domains theories. As evident, there is no one theory or "magic bullet" that can account for the phenomenon. Further, the theories appear to overlap significantly and, perhaps in conjunction, may provide a more complete explanation of the dropout phenomenon. Perez and Salazar (1997) note that the various factors discussed herein in isolation may not be the cause of students leaving school because there may be other intervening factors; they mention family socioeconomic status and other aspects of family background as possible intervening factors.

Contextual factors theoretically and empirically appear to be important influences on academic outcome. Ianni and Orr (1996) note the special importance of context in their discussion; in closing, they point out that structural deficits across the domains of school, family, and community seem to be the most significant causes for dropping out of high school in high-poverty areas, whereas adolescent development, social role behavior, and culture conflict are more likely to be explanatory causes of student drop out in the absence of pronounced structural deficits. As evident, the causal factors of early school exit are rather complex. They point, however, to the necessity of investigating both contextual and intra-psychic processes. Therefore, a holistic framework is necessary to adopt, one that views adolescent development as imbedded within a sociocultural milieu.

In total, the theories view the dropout phenomenon from a deficit perspective. As previously argued, such theories tell us very little about what promotes resilience and development in ethnic youth. Further, they cannot account for individual differences or for differences in developmental trajectories. For example, the theories are ineffective at explaining why it is that some youth, despite an at-risk status, reveal an academic and developmental trajectory of competence rather than incompetence. Therefore, an exploration of models of resilience is in order for the purpose of understanding such phenomenon at greater depth.

ACADEMIC RESILIENCE

In general, resilience, as an area of inquiry and study, is increasingly gaining popularity both in scientific endeavors as well as in the media. This recent historical shift from a deficit model perspective to a strength model perspective in understanding complex phenomenon is particularly noteworthy and may be extremely productive. For example, focusing on the shortcomings of students who are at risk of academic failure may provide us with very little information about how to promote development or growth; whereas a focus on the factors that account for success may help us to identify and enhance those factors that moderate the influence of risk factors on outcomes (see Gonzalez & Padilla, 1997). A practical implication of this knowledge may be in the design of prevention and intervention programs that promote academic resilience in at-risk populations.

Resilience is understood within a context of risk. Gonzalez and Padilla (1997) affirm that to be identified as resilient, one must be at risk of negative outcomes. Alva (1991) similarly notes that academically resilient students are described as students "who sustain high levels of achievement, motivation and performance despite the presence of stressful events and conditions that place them at risk of doing poorly in school and ultimately dropping out of school" (p. 19).

Risk factors for ethnic youth include minority status, discrimination, alienating schools, economic hardship, difficulty understanding the English language, or having parents who are unfamiliar with the education system in the U.S. (cited in Gonzalez & Padilla, 1997).

Persistency is another frequently mentioned attribute of academically successful students (see Valencia, 1994). Two interpretations of this term are found in the literature; one referring to staying in school versus dropping out, and the other referring to personal attributes of academically oriented students. Students who are goal oriented (e.g., degree attainment, access to better jobs, and higher incomes) and who have high academic competence, a positive self-concept, a realistic self-appraisal, the ability to deal with racism, the availability of a strong support person, participation in extracurricular activities, and who are involved in their communities have been found to reveal greater academic persistence than those who do not possess these personal and environmental resources (see Valencia, 1994).

However, the research findings appear to contradict each other. For example, some studies have found that only high academic ability and goal commitment were predictors of academic achievement and persistency for minority youth, specifically, for African-American and Mexican-American students (see Arbona & Novy, 1990), whereas other studies have provided support for the relevance of multiple personal and environmental variables as predictors of academic persistence (see Valencia, 1994).

Academic resilience and persistence are related constructs in that they both may be seen to contribute importantly to academic success. For example, Gandara (1995) found that family support and individual persistence were the factors that contributed most to Chicana/o students' academic success (see below). Familial support has been found to be an important predictor of academic resilience in a study by Gonzalez and Padilla (1997). A number of studies point to the importance of resiliency factors in ethnic minorities' trajectories of academic success (see the review noted below). Moreover, the two constructs may be distinguished in that persistence appears to be an important personal attribute that may significantly contribute to academic success, whereas academic resilience refers to both personal and environmental resources that contribute to school success within a context of risk.

As discussed above, both Latina/o and Southeast Asian youth have been identified in the literature as significantly economically stressed which may place them at risk of academic failure. Low socioeconomic status (SES) is particularly problematic and has been strongly and consistently associated with poor academic performance (see National Research Council, 1993). However, as also discussed, not all youth, despite similar socioeconomic backgrounds, succumb to school failure.

There are those who are able to rise above diversity despite an at-risk status. What are the characteristics of such youths and what factors promote success for at-risk youth? To gain a better understanding of resilience in general, an overview of the general models of resilience will be undertaken, followed by a more thorough discussion of resilience and persistence in the academic sphere across the populations of interest (i.e., Latina/o and Southeast Asian).

Certain models have been proposed in the literature in an effort to understand the complex relationships among stress, risk, and resilience. The contextual model of stress, risk, and resilience has as its goal an understanding of the stress process by taking into account the personal circumstances or contexts in which stressful events or transitions occur (Gore & Eckenrode, 1996). Evidence indicates that some types of stress have salutary effects on development. For example, Elder (1974) found that family hardships propelled older boys who experienced the Great Depression into early social independence and Weiss (1979) found that teenage children in single-parent families tend to "grow up faster," developing a "new salutary motivation" that comes from helping the single parent (Gore & Eckenrode, 1996).

Examples such as these illustrate how an at-risk status and the effects of certain stressors imposed on the family challenge all members and may spur the growth of adolescents, a process referred to as the "accentuation process" because the stressor emphasizes the healthy tendencies already present within the environment (Gore & Eckenrode, 1996). In sum, the contextual model is noteworthy because it considers the multi-dimensional nature of stressors and offers a means of understanding the interrelationships of various factors within differing sociocultural contexts.

Another theory utilized for understanding the relationships among stress, risk, and resilience is the stress mediation model. The general idea of the theory is that the magnitude of the stressor-mental health relationship may be attenuated if protective processes "buffer" stress effects (Gore & Eckenrode, 1996; Haggerty, Sherrod, Garmezy, & Rutter, 1996; Werner & Smith, 1982). Protective factors or "buffers" are hypothesized to reduce the likelihood of dysfunction in the presence of vulnerabilities and stressful life experiences (Gore & Eckenrode, 1996; Haggerty, Sherrod, Garmezy, & Rutter, 1996; Werner & Smith, 1982). These protective factors have been generally categorized into two broad dimensions: (1) personal resources such as temperament, physical health status, self-esteem, motivation, and mastery; and (2) environmental resources such as family income, social support (Gore & Eckenrode, 1996), students' beliefs, values, and attitudes toward education, the quality of their student-teacher interactions, the general school climate (Arellano & Padilla, 1996), teacher expectations and affirmations, and positive school experiences validating the students' success (Alva & Padilla, 1995).

Elsewhere, protective factors have been divided into the following three categories: (1) attributes of the individual, including resilient temperament, positive social orientation and activity level, accurate processing of interpersonal cues, good means-ends problem solving skills, an ability to evaluate alternative actions from both instrumental and affective perspectives, the capacity to enact behaviors that accomplish desired outcomes in interpersonal or social situations, and a sense of self-efficacy; (2) a supportive family environment, including bonding with adults in the family, low family conflict, and supportive relationships; and (3) environmental supports, including those which reinforce and support coping efforts and recognize and reward competence (Garmezy, 1985; Lerner & Vicary, 1984; Rutter, 1980, 1985; Werner, 1989). Evidence in support of such protective factors may be gleaned from numerous studies (e.g., Egeland, Breitenbucher, & Rosenberg, 1980; Garmezy, Masten, & Tellegen, 1984; Rutter & Quinton, 1984; Werner & Smith, 1982).

Rutter (1987) believes that such factors may be protective if they exert a moderating effect on the influence of a risk factor. Protective processes have been found empirically to serve the following moderating functions: (1) reduction of risk impact, including processes that alter the risk or the person's exposure to the risk; (2) reduction of negative chain reactions that follow exposure to the threatening effect and contribute to long-term effects of exposure; (3) self-esteem and self-efficacy, developed through personal relationships, new experiences, and task accomplishment; and (4) opening up of opportunity, processes that permit the individual to gain access to resources or to complete important life transitions (Nettles & Pleck, 1996).

Further, Arellano and Padilla (1996) state that resilience depends upon the "goodness-of-fit" between environmental resources or contextual events, such as family or school experiences, and access to personal adaptive resources, such as a sense of self-efficacy, when events conflict. Gore and Eckenrode (1996) caution the reader to not view these personal and environmental factors in isolation but rather to view them as interconnected. Further, they argue that protective factors may combine in non-additive ways in producing protective effects (also see Rutter, 1987). They offer the example of self-esteem and social support to illustrate this phenomenon. Research has found that these factors are indeed related, further they have been found to vary in relation to each other (see Gore & Eckenrode, 1996). Lastly, the authors argue that temporal issues also need to be considered. They point out that the presence of certain protective factors may determine the emergence of other protective mechanisms at some later time.

In sum, the two models (i.e., personal and environment) discussed above in conjunction appear to offer the best possible conceptualization of the multi-faceted nature of resilience and for differences in academic trajectories for at-risk ethnic youth. For example, a context of adversity such as poverty may spur some youth with other resources (e.g., familial social support) to adopt growth enhancing strategies (e.g., academic achievement) for personal and/or familial motivation, whereas for youth not blessed with additional resources, a trajectory of academic failure may be more apparent.

Latina/o Academic Outcomes

A number of studies have been conducted on the concept of academic resilience in Latinas/os. These studies converge on the importance of investigating both personal and sociocultural factors in understanding resilience. For example, focusing on both personal and sociocultural factors, Alva (1991) found in a sample of 384 Mexican American sophomores in a predominantly Hispanic (78%) high school in Los

Angeles county that students' subjective appraisal of their preparation for college was the most significant predictor of GPA and that educational support from teachers and friends plus a sense of control over one's academic future predicted high GPA (cited in Gonzalez & Padilla, 1997).

Immigrant status was also argued to be a protective factor for ethnic youth. In Rumbaut's (2000) previously discussed multi-ethnic Children of Immigrants Longitudinal Study (CILS), data revealed an interesting resilience paradox evident for both immigrant youth and females. Even though the more recently arrived foreign-born youths invested more effort in their school work and revealed higher GPAs, they nevertheless exhibited lower self-esteem and higher depressive symptoms than their U.S.-born counterparts. Females also evidenced a similar pattern of greater effort and academic achievement with concomitant psychological effects, which Rumbaut argues is a manifestation of the devalued and disparaged social status of these groups in our society. Apparently, the relationship between immigrant status (and female status) and resilience is complex. It appears to promote resilience in some venues (i.e., academic) but may be a liability in others (i.e., social status).

Goodenow (1992) found in her multi-ethnic study of the impact of a psychological sense of school membership on school achievement that low SES Hispanic junior high school students, who felt a sense of belonging to the school environment, were more engaged and exhibited greater effort on academic tasks, which resulted in greater acceptance and belonging from others in that environment (cited in Gonzalez & Padilla, 1997). Elaborating on these findings, Hernandez (1993) found in his Pueblo, Colorado, sample of low SES high school students that extracurricular activities increased a student's sense of engagement within the school, which in turn served as a protective factor to ameliorate negative outcomes (cited in Gonzalez & Padilla, 1997). Another factor investigated by Hernandez was the role of social support in academic resilience. Hernandez found that teacher support, peer instrumental support, and parent motivational support all contributed to academic achievement among resilient students.

Further support of the importance of both personal and sociocultural factors in resilience comes from a recent study by Gonzalez and Padilla (1997). Their sample was selected from a database of 2,169 Mexican American students in three California high schools with high concentrations of Mexicans and Mexican-Americans. The researchers utilized self-reported grades to distinguish high-achieving or resilient students and low-achieving or non-resilient students. Further, 133 students comprised the resilient category, while 81 students comprised the non-resilient category.

The researchers found that certain characteristics distinguished resilient from non-resilient students. Resilient students in their study were more likely to be female, to have immigrant parents, to have been born outside of the U.S., to have foreign schooling, to be tracked in college preparatory classes, to attend ethnically homogeneous schools, and to live with both parents. Non-resilient students were more likely to live with their mothers only, to have parents with lower educational levels, and were more likely to be sophomores in high school. The researchers found that both a supportive academic environment and a student's subjective appraisal of the school environment were important factors that influenced academic resilience. Specifically, a sense of belonging to school, family and peer support, familialism, and value placed on school were significant predictors of academic resilience. Gonzalez and Padilla concluded that a sense of belonging to school enhances resilience and that academic resilience is influenced by cultural factors.

A potential confounder in this study may be generational status, however. It appears that the researchers sampled from two distinct populations: an immigrant population and a more established population. Consequently, the differences between these two groups may disappear after controlling for generational status. Nevertheless, this study is noteworthy in that a cultural value (i.e., familialism) was found to be a significant predictor of academic resilience. It would be interesting to investigate whether this and the other findings hold in a heterogeneous school population. Gonzalez and Padilla believe that living in an ethnic enclave (primarily Hispanic) may help foster a socially supportive climate. However, not all communities have similarly high concentrations of Hispanics. In many communities, Hispanics do not constitute the majority of the residents; consequently, there may be less support available for Hispanic youth.

However, in Gandara's (1995) study resilient Mexican American females all attended integrated schools. She was one of the first researchers who attempted to explain the academic resilience of at-risk

Mexican Americans or Chicanas/os. In her retrospective, qualitative study of 50 high achieving, disadvantaged Chicanos, Gandara (1995) found that a number of personal and sociocultural factors characterized this sample. First and foremost for the purposes of this study, most subjects could be described as biculturally competent. The overwhelmingly majority of them came from homes where Spanish was the primary language. Gandara described the sample as "additive bilinguals" or "individuals who build a second language onto the firm foundation of a first, so that they continue to develop linguistically and cognitively in both languages" (p. 89). Her finding substantiates the literature that finds that biculturality enhances rather than detracts from competence (see the section on bicultural competence for further elaboration on this phenomenon).

Persistence was an intrapersonal factor cited by most subjects as a key characteristic of their success. A number of researchers support the notion that persistence plays an important role in academic achievement and attainment. For example, Simonton (1987) found that persistence was more powerful than ability by itself in explaining the accomplishments of a sample of outstanding achievers (cited in Gandara, 1995). These researchers do not discount the influence of intelligence; but they do, however, point out that other characteristics also factor importantly in academic achievement and attainment. Apparently, intelligence alone is not sufficient to account for successful performance in this domain.

Persistence is thought to develop from a "self-belief of efficacy," thought to be engendered by experiences of mastery, modeling behavior, and social persuasion (Gandara, 1995). According to Bandura (1990), it is this self-belief of efficacy that determines how much a person will persevere in the face of obstacles and how much effort a person will exert in an endeavor (cited in Gandara, 1995). Bandura calls this a resilient self-belief system, which enables a person to rise above adversity. Gandara's sample obviously had a strong self-belief system. They accomplished much educationally, earning a Ph.D., J.D., or M.D., despite their impoverished backgrounds.

Also, Gandara found that 60 percent of the high achievers were judged to be light skinned or European looking, although interestingly most considered themselves to look "typically Mexican." Much research confirms the observation that lighter skin color affords greater opportunities for individuals. Lighter skin color has been found in numerous studies to correlate with enhanced life chances and earnings, decreased discrimination, increased occupational mobility, and increased educational attainment (Gandara, 1995). Gandara concludes that phenotype may be related to opportunity structure and discrimination in the U.S.

Gandara also noted significant gender differences in the sample. Most female high achievers were consistently good students who tended to aspire to college early in their school careers; whereas the male high achievers revealed a more uneven picture of academic development, sometimes delaying their decision to attend college (Gandara, 1995). Apparently, academic aspirations may be a significant factor for educational attainment for females but may not be so for males.

Regarding sociocultural factors, Gandara found that most subjects reported that their parents stressed the development of independence and training in responsibility throughout their formative years. Researchers concur "that motivation for achievement could be engendered in children through early training by setting high standards and providing sufficient independence for the child to develop a sense of task mastery" (Gandara, 1995, p. 27). Parents of the sample appeared to create an "achievement press" in their homes for higher academic performance, despite the lack of economic resources and familiarity with the second culture. They appeared to achieve this through the value of perseverance and a strong work ethic.

Other home influences also figured importantly on academic outcome in Gandara's sample. Parental influence on academic and career decision-making has been found to be significantly greater for Hispanic youth than for non-Hispanic youth (Gandara, 1995). Parental support, especially mothers' support, was an especially powerful and guiding force in the subjects' educational ambitions. This support most often came in the form of verbal support and encouragement. Parents of these high achievers also held high aspirations for their children which has been found in the literature to predict similar aspirations in one's children, but most parents of the sample, however, aspired to nothing higher than a high school education for their children, although they accomplished much more (Gandara, 1995). Also, a high premium was placed on ideas and information (e.g., reading materials) in the homes of these high achievers, in spite of the very limited formal education and economic resources of the parents (Gandara, 1995). Parents who could not provide intellectual stimulation for their children supported their children's education via other routes, such as protecting their study time and settling down to live in one place.

Regarding school influences, research has found that schools have a greater impact on minority student achievement than on the achievement of white students (Gandara, 1995). Schools exert their influence on students via the teachers, student body, and curriculum routes (Gandara, 1995). High academic achievement is correlated in the literature with attending middle- to upper-middle-class, racially integrated schools and attending schools where teachers hold high academic standards and expectations for all students (Gandara, 1995). Regarding the sample, most of the parents and subjects themselves opted for Catholic educations, which took them outside of the barrio. They financed this education via the support of the Catholic Church and their relatives. More than two-thirds of the subjects attended middle- to upper-middle-class, Anglo schools. Further, all of them found themselves in college-bound courses through their persistence and determination.

Finally, research has found that peers influence achievement behavior (see Epstein & Karweit, 1983; Steinberg et al., 1988). Researchers have found that students whose school friends are high achievers also tend to be high achievers themselves, and students whose school friends are at-risk of dropping out also are at-risk of dropping out themselves (Gandara, 1995). Gandara points out that high achievement in school may be a liability for Latino students in inner city schools. Some Latino students may fear that they will be labeled as "White" by their peers if they succeed academically. They may be caught in a double bind— fearing alienation from their peers and feeling pressured to resist the dominant culture via identification with an oppositional culture. Apparently, peer influence appears to be a notable challenge to conceptualizations of the self or identity formation for such youths. For example, some youth, who are anxious for approval and self-definition, may succumb to negative peer pressure. Yet there are others who do not succumb to such pressures and who do not sacrifice the integrity of their developing identities.

Most of Gandara's subjects managed to succeed both academically and socially without insult to their developing identities. Gandara attributes this success in balancing friendships with school performance to a number of factors. A significant sociocultural factor that figured importantly in the lives and successes of these youths was the influence of protective factors. Protective factors have been studied extensively in the literature and have been found to shield children from the potentially negative effects of an at-risk status, as previously noted (also see Rutter, 1979; Werner & Smith, 1989).

Gandara found that most of her subjects enjoyed the protection of the following three protective factors: (1) a positive relationship with at least one caring adult, (2) the communication of high expectations for the child, and (3) and opportunities to participate meaningfully in family or group endeavors (also see Bernard, 1991).

Gandara also notes the significant influence of intrapersonal factors implicated in the youths' successful negotiation in these domains. Gandara believes that the subjects of her study successfully negotiated "dual identities" or reference groups. Mehan, Hubbard, and Villanueva (1994) found a similar phenomenon in their participants of the AVID (Advancement via Individual Determination) program. These authors attributed this phenomenon to the development of an ideology that is neither oppositional nor conformist, but rather one that combines elements of both achievement and cultural affirmation or the equivalent of an "accommodation without assimilation" belief system (cited in Gandara, 1995).

This phenomenon also has been referred to as "additive acculturation." Gibson (1993) elaborates on this phenomenon in the following:

> Recent studies show that many first and second generation immigrant children are successful not because they relinquish their traditional ways but because they draw strength from their home cultures and a positive sense of their ethnic identity. They distinguish the acquisition of school skills and the gaining of proficiency in the ways of the mainstream from their own social identification with a particular ethnic group (p.7).

The researcher So (1987) found in his study of high-achieving, low-income, Hispanic students from the "High School and Beyond" data set, that their subjects were found to have dual reference groups or to be identified with both middle-class values and their own ethnic group (cited in Gandara, 1995). So found that "those who aspire to the middle class, as well as maintain strong communicative skills within the Hispanic culture, outperform those who do not aspire to the middle class and do not maintain strong communicative skills with their parents and reference group . . . [A] high achieving disadvantaged student can retain minority group identity while at the same time aspiring to membership in the middle class" (pp. 30-31).

Most of Gandara's subjects successfully maintained two separate peer groups: one at school and one at home. These subjects were adept at moving between the two cultures: in the high achieving Anglo context of their schools and in the disadvantaged, poverty-stricken barrios of their neighborhoods. They accomplished this without alienating their communities or sacrificing the integrity of their identities. This phenomenon, also referred to in the literature as bicultural competence, will be elaborated on in the following chapter.

Southeast Asian Academic Outcomes

Far fewer studies have been conducted on academic resilience in Southeast Asian students. Most studies that have investigated this construct tend to treat Asian Americans as a homogenous population, lumping the various subcultures into one category. Such studies usually point out that Asian Americans often surpass the academic achievement of American students. However, as previously noted, the various Asian American subcultures are culturally, socially, and economically distinct; therefore academic outcomes may differ markedly across the subcultural groups.

To illustrate this tendency, a discussion of several current studies in the literature which highlight this critical research flaw will follow. For example, Fuligni (1997) found in his multi-ethnic study that East Asian students significantly out-performed Latino (i.e., Mexican, Central and South American) students academically; in fact, East Asian students attained the highest course grades while the Latino students received the lowest. Further, Fuligni found that in his first and second generation sample that only a small portion of their success could be attributed to their socioeconomic background (e.g., parents' education); a more significant correlate of their achievement was a strong emphasis on education that was shared by the students, their parents, and peers. Fuligni notes that successful students consistently indicated higher values of schooling and educational success, and expended substantially more time and effort on academic endeavors.

However, the majority of his East Asian students reported being of Chinese descent while the minority indicated Korean, Indian, and Southeast Asian backgrounds. Thus, the contribution of the Southeast Asian group to this sample appears minimal. Unfortunately, the ethnic breakdown of the Southeast Asian group was not reported. Thus, we do not know what particular Southeast Asian groups composed this sample. Further, it is quite possible that the study findings may be confounded by inequivalence within this sample. These various Asian groups may conceivably be very different from one another in terms of academic achievement, for example. Furthermore, since the Chinese students constitute the majority of the sample, their scores may substantially inflate the findings to such a degree that low scores from the other subcultural groups may make a negligible difference in the study findings.

Alva (1993) similarly grouped the various Asian American subcultural groups into one category in her study of achievement among Asian American adolescents. In her sample of 89 urban 10th grade high school students, Alva found that Asian American students whose educational and social experiences convey a strong link between schooling, academic success, and social integration were more likely to demonstrate patterns of achievement, as reflected in higher grades and better performance on standardized tests. Similar to the Latina/o findings, Asian American students who felt greater involvement in school activities were more likely to receive higher grades which suggests that academically successful students are more socially integrated and feel a sense of identification with school (Alva, 1993).

In conjunction, both studies also point to the importance of personal and sociocultural factors in academic resilience. However, the studies are confounded substantially by the inherent inequivalence of the subcultural groups that constitute the sample. Some theorists and researchers have attempted to address such issues. For example, Blair and Qian (1998) discussed the diversity found within this supracategory. They pointed out that contrary to the popular stereotype of Asian Americans as the "model minority", not all Asian Americans achieve unprecedented success in terms of educational performance and attainment. These researchers assert that although Southeast Asian families place a high premium on their children's educational achievements, they nevertheless encounter many difficulties in this regard. They note that many Southeast Asian parents may seek to maintain their respective cultural practices to such an extent that it impedes their children's participation in certain educational activities such as involvement in extracurricular school activities. Further, these researchers note that many parents from Southeast Asia tend to have less education than other Asian groups, and may lack a cultural understanding of American norms and the English language, to the extent that they cannot offer their children much educational support.

In sum, the research findings appear to point to the importance of both personal and sociocultural factors as predictors of academic resilience. Personal factors, such as a sense of connectedness to school and academic values, and sociocultural factors, such as parental support and value placed on school, may be significant predictors of academic performance across the two cultural groups (i.e., Latina/o and Southeast Asian). Further, the research findings appear to suggest that bicultural competence may be a significant personal predictor of academic resilience, at least for Latinas/os. Unfortunately, the role of this factor in the academic outcome of Southeast Asians is unknown. In general, much more is known about the predictors of academic success in Latina/o adolescents than in the Southeast Asian youth. Furthermore, the few studies that focus on this construct are seriously confounded by not accounting for the heterogeneity found within Asian American subcultural groups (e.g., differences in generational status and socioeconomic status). More carefully conducted studies that focus on the predictors of academic outcomes, specifically in Southeast Asian youth, are needed. Furthermore, the role of bicultural competence in academic outcomes needs to be elaborated on across cultures.

CHAPTER 3

The Construction of Bicultural Competence

BICULTURAL COMPETENCE

[F]or the full and equal participation of language minorities in American society requires not that these groups try to become indistinguishable from the white majority, but rather that they strengthen themselves from within—culturally, socially, politically, and economically. . . Academically prepared individuals who are alienated from their community and who are culturally adrift cannot be assets either to themselves or to society.
-Hernandez-Chavez (1984, p. 170-171).

Acculturation

The process of culture contact and cultural change is a continuing saga of human history. The construct of acculturation refers to this process. Acculturation has been defined as a cultural exchange that results from continuous first-hand contact between two distinct cultural groups (Redfield, Linton, & Herskovits, 1936). Acculturation has been noted in the literature to occur across multiple levels. Graves (1967) distinguished acculturation on a group or collective level from acculturation on an individual or psychological level. From this perspective, acculturation is seen as both a change in the culture of the group as well as a change in the psychology of the individual. This distinction is important because individuals differ in the degree to which they participate in their cultural group's changes (see Berry, 1970; Furnham & Bochner, 1986). Further, groups also differ in their rates of changes. Some groups acculturate more quickly than others (see Berry, 1970; Furnham & Bochner, 1986). What accounts for these differences in rates of change and what exactly changes?

Acculturation does not occur uniformly across the two groups in contact. Usually, there is more pressure for the less dominant group to change than for the dominant group (see Berry, 1990). Berry notes that the more dominant group pressures the less dominant group to acculturate (for a thorough discussion of these group dynamics, the reader is referred to Berry, 1990). Berry notes that the more dominant group pressures the less dominant group to acculturate. Trimble (2003) notes that cultural groups possess unique "eidos" and "ethos" or "lifeways" and "thoughtways." An example of an eidos may be familial obligation (e.g., providing material, emotional, or social support to family) while an example of an ethos may be optimism in the face of adversity. Permanent changes to an individual's eidos and ethos may occur in the course of interaction between cultural groups.

As aforementioned, cultural change occurs across multiple levels. Currently, acculturation is viewed as a bidirectional and multidimensional phenomena (see Chun, Balls Organista, & Marin, 2003). Previously, acculturation and assimilation were posited to be synonymous or that assimilation is the inevitable outcome of acculturation (i.e., the unidirectional argument). We now understand that immigrant populations adopt aspects of the host's culture that are concordant with their original worldview while preserving elements of their traditional culture. Regarding multidimensionality, change occurs on the physical, biological, political, economic, cultural, social, and psychological levels (see Berry, 1991). Physically, an individual may encounter changes in dwelling arrangements and exposure to environmental pollutants, for example. On a biological level, individuals may encounter changes in nutritional status and exposure to new diseases. Political changes may involve the oppression of the non-dominant group by the dominant group, for example. Economically, acculturating individuals may experience a loss of traditional means of survival and the introduction of different, sometimes alien forms of employment, for example, from the weaving of traditional textiles on a loom in one's home to the sewing of uniforms on a sewing machine in a sweatshop.

Cultural changes include linguistic, religious, or educational shifts. Acculturating individuals may encounter the additional stress of learning a new language, for example. Social changes may include the loss of traditional forms of social support and/or exposure to new kinds of relationships, such as participation in subordinate/dominant relational patterns. Lastly, on a psychological level, changes in values, identities, abilities, and motives may occur. For example, some individuals may develop a bicultural identity as a consequence of exposure to new or different cultural contexts, incorporating elements of a culture into their schema of the self. Sometimes, a unique identity may emerge, which is distinct from both the traditional ethnic and the dominant group's identity formulations (see Bicultural Competence). Further, individuals may vary in their strategies and abilities to integrate diverse cultural systems (see Bicultural Competence).

In sum, as is evident, the construct of acculturation is multidimensional, involving change across multiple levels. Moreover, the groups in contact with each other do not change equally, but rather, one group, the "acculturating group," may make the greatest changes, whereas the other group, the "dominant group," may be seen to enforce change on the acculturating group by providing economic incentives (i.e., better jobs), for example (see Berry, 1990). Acculturation is not necessarily a negative phenomenon. The prevalent conceptualization appears to support the notion that socio-psychological outcomes are highly variable, depending upon personal and environmental characteristics (Berry, 1998). Further, individual members of cultural groups vary in their motivation and ability to make such changes.

Theoretical Models of Second-Culture Acquisition

According to Berry (1991), individuals may adopt various different strategies of cultural change. Berry discusses four major types of acculturation strategies, as follows: (1) the assimilation strategy, which is characterized by rejection of one's ethnic culture while embracing the new or different culture(s); (2) the separation strategy, which is characterized by rejection or avoidance of the new or different culture(s) while maintaining one's original culture; (3) the integration option, which is characterized by maintenance of one's original culture while in daily interaction with the other culture(s); and (4) the marginalization alternative, which is characterized by a lack of interest in maintaining one's original culture, as well as little interest in the new or different culture(s). Adoption of a particular strategy over another is contingent on a number of factors, such as life events (see Berry's model, Figure 4-1, in Chapter 4).

Thus, it appears that individuals may adopt a number of different strategies as they navigate different cultural milieus. However, these strategies do not inform us of their ramifications on development. Therefore, a discussion of models of acculturation will follow, which synthesizes behavioral strategies with specific assumptions and developmental consequences.

A related construct to acculturation is second-culture acquisition. The following five models of second-culture acquisition have been explored in the literature: (1) the assimilation, (2) the acculturation, (3) the multiculturalism, (4) the fusion, and (5) the alternation models. Each model is believed to embrace a slightly different set of assumptions, and each is said to focus on different outcomes for the individual (LaFromboise, Coleman, & Gerton, 1993).

The assimilation model, as discussed above, posits an ongoing process of absorption into the culture that is perceived as dominant or more desirable. The underlying assumption of this model is that a member of one culture loses her/he original cultural identity as she/he acquires a new identity in a second culture. This process is associated with a number of negative consequences, for example, a sense of alienation and isolation, social difficulties, stress and anxiety for the individual, etc.

The acculturation model differs from the assimilation model in that the individual, while becoming a competent participant in the majority culture, will always be identified as a member of the minority culture. Further, this process is thought to be a stressful experience—both economically and psychologically—because it reinforces second-class citizenship and alienation of the individual acclimating to a new culture.

The multicultural model promotes a pluralistic approach to understanding the relationship between two or more cultures. It posits the possibility that cultures may maintain distinct identities, while individuals from one culture work with those of other cultures to serve common national or economic needs. However, LaFromboise, Coleman, and Gerton are skeptical about this model, pointing to the inherent difficulty in maintaining a truly multicultural society over time, but believe instead that it is more likely that the various groups will intermingle, thus leading to the evolution of a new culture.

The fusion model of second-culture acquisition posits that cultures sharing an economic, political, or geographic space will fuse together until they are indistinguishable to form a new culture. However, in the case of this model, the researchers also are skeptical, stating that there are few successful examples of such a new culture. Furthermore, they assert that it is the minority groups that become assimilated into the majority group at the price of their ethnic identities.

On the other hand, the alternation model is associated with a number of positive outcomes. It assumes that it is possible for an individual to know and understand two different cultures as well as to alter one's behavior to fit a particular social context. The model postulates that an individual can choose the degree and manner to which she/he will affiliate with either the second culture or her/his culture of origin, and that it is possible to maintain a positive relationship with both. Another assumption of the model is that it is possible for an individual to have a sense of belonging in two cultures without compromising one's sense of cultural identity. A bicultural orientation is believed to evolve from this model.

Further, bicultural individuals are believed to use different problem-solving, coping, human relational, communication, and incentive motivational styles, depending on the demands of the social context (also see Ramirez, 1984). Some authors have speculated that individuals who have the ability to effectively alternate their use of culturally appropriate behavior may exhibit less stress and anxiety, higher cognitive functioning and mental health status than people who are mono-cultural, assimilated, or acculturated (cited in LaFromboise, Coleman, & Gerton, 1993). Adler (1975) has argued that an outcome of the alternation model may be an enhanced intuitive, emotional, and cognitive experience (cited in LaFromboise, Coleman, & Gerton, 1993).

The alternation model differs from the assimilation and acculturation models in the following ways: (1) it posits a bidirectional and orthogonal relationship between the individual's culture of origin and the second culture in which she/he may be living in rather than the linear and unidirectional relationship of the other two models; and (2) it does not assume a hierarchical relationship between two cultures; in other words, it is possible to assign equal status to the two cultures, even if one does not value them equally (LaFromboise, Coleman, & Gerton, 1993).

In sum, each model has its own assumptions concerning the process of second-culture acquisition. Further, the models are believed to be not mutually exclusive; each one may represent an adequate explanation for a person's experience as she acquires competency in a new culture; however, most of the models, with the notable exception of the alternation model, assume that an individual will lose identification with her culture of origin, a process believed to be stressful and disorienting (LaFromboise, Coleman, & Gerton, 1993). However, as previously noted, the acculturation process does not inevitably entail the development of social and psychological problems. Variable outcomes have been found in the literature, depending upon individual and environmental factors. Some acculturate with relative ease while others experience more conflict or "culture shock" throughout this process (for a thorough discussion of this phenomenon see Berry, 1998; also see Berry's model, Figure 4-1, in Chapter 4).

Since the phenomenon of bicultural competence is of relevance to this study, the discussion will focus on those processes that promote psychological, behavioral, cognitive, and social adaptation to a diverse cultural milieu. Therefore, the alternation model appears to be the superior model to explain bicultural competence. Its essential strength is believed to lie in its focus on the cognitive and affective processes that allow an individual to withstand the negative impact of acculturative stress. Also, it appears to be an excellent model to explain how situational factors may interact with personal factors to influence outcome (e.g., academic resilience).

Bicultural Competence

Ramirez (1983) defines biculturalism as an integration of the competencies and sensitivities associated with two cultures within a person (cited in Buriel et al., 1998). Biculturalism typically refers to minority youths' exposure to the majority culture and to the degree that youths then associate themselves with the majority culture (Rotheram-Borus, 1993). Suarez, Fowers, Garwood, and Szapocznik (1997) note that biculturalism develops along two independent dimensions involving a linear process of accommodation to the host culture on one dimension, and on the other, a complex process by which an individual maintains some values and attachments to the culture of origin while modifying others (also see Szapocznik & Kurtines, 1980).

According to Buriel et al. (1998), biculturalism is considered to be an optimum cultural adaptation strategy for Latinos and other non-Western immigrant groups who must respond to the often competing demands of two cultural systems (also see Harrison, Wilson, Pine, Chan, & Buriel, 1990; LaFromboise, Coleman, & Gerton, 1993: Ramirez, 1983). Further, biculturalism has been found to be greater in immigrant families and in first and second-generation children of immigrants (see Buriel, 1993).

Rotheram-Borus (1993) states that adolescents may engage in the following decision-making process when faced with such a situation: they may either choose to closely identify with mainstream culture, to strongly identify with one's own ethnic group, or to opt for a bicultural orientation. As evident, biculturalism is strongly related to ethnic identity. Rotheram-Borus states that ethnic identity is reflected in how youths choose to label themselves, the role models they identify with, and the norms and values they endorse. Further, adolescents' ethnic identity is strongly influenced by context (see Rotheram-Borus, 1993). Biculturals are then characterized as youths who have been exposed to multiple groups and who have chosen a bicultural orientation (see Rotheram-Borus, 1993).

As evident, a number of terms are used in the literature to describe biculturalism. These terms are bicultural identity, bicultural self-identification, bicultural reference group orientation, and bicultural competence. It is easy to confuse the terminology because they appear to be related to each other and are sometimes used interchangeably in the literature. However, some theorists and researchers clearly distinguish amongst these constructs, positing different phenomena and outcomes for each. For example, Rotheram-Borus argues that a bicultural reference group orientation, the group of the youth's choice, and bicultural competence, referring to behavioral routines, are more salient constructs for youth than bicultural identity and bicultural self-identification, which are later emerging phenomena, typically consolidated in adulthood (also see Phinney, 1993). It is outside the scope of this review to discuss these various associated constructs in depth. Herein, the focus of the discussion will be on the construct of bicultural competence because of its relevance for the study.

The construct of bicultural competence as a result of living in two cultures grows out of the alternation model (LaFromboise, Coleman, & Gerton, 1993). These theorists believe that psychological well-being for bicultural individuals lies in the ability to develop and maintain competence in both cultures, whereas other researchers point out that this construct refers to the ability to function effectively in multiple ethnic or pluralistic environments (see Rotheram-Borus, 1993).

Further, Rotheram-Borus points out that bicultural competence refers to an understanding of the varying social norms of at least two groups. However, other theorists suggest multiple areas in which the bicultural individual must develop competencies for positive outcomes (see LaFromboise et al., 1993).

LaFromboise, Coleman, and Gerton argue that for the development of bicultural competence, the following individual characteristics are considered significant. These characteristics include, but are not limited to: personal identity (e.g., a certain degree of individuation, self awareness, and ego strength), cultural identity (e.g., a strong sense of oneself in relation to others), age and life stage, gender and gender role identification, and socioeconomic status.

To achieve bicultural competence, they suggest the following dimensions in which an individual may need to develop competency so as to effectively manage the process of living in two cultures. The dimensions are as follows: (1) knowledge of cultural beliefs and values of both the second culture and the culture of origin, (2) positive attitudes toward both majority and minority groups, (3) bicultural efficacy, which refers to the belief or confidence that one can live effectively and in a satisfying manner within two groups without compromising one's sense of cultural identity, (4) communication ability, which refers to an individual's effectiveness in communicating ideas and feelings to members of a given culture, both verbally and nonverbally, (5) role repertoire, which refers to the range of culturally or situationally appropriate behaviors or roles an individual has developed; the greater the range of behaviors or roles, the higher the level of cultural competence, and (6) a sense of being grounded, which refers to the establishment of stable social networks in both cultures.

In sum, for bicultural competence, it is believed that an individual must achieve and maintain a certain set of skills (see above). Ethnic minority individuals who develop these skills are believed to have better physical and psychological health than those who do not (LaFromboise, Coleman, & Gerton,1993). Although this phenomenon appears to be associated with a number of positive outcomes, the empirical data are inconsistent. Some studies support the theory, while others find no associations or report contradictory results (see Bicultural Competence and Academic Outcomes). Also, many studies that have assessed this phenomenon are methodologically flawed (see Bicultural Competence and Academic Outcomes); therefore the findings are inconclusive.

While bicultural competence may enhance resilience in general, it is not yet clear whether this construct will specifically promote academic resilience, nor is it clear in which manner this construct may promote resilience in this domain. Further, this construct appears to be linked to stress and coping processes; however, this relationship is not clearly understood in the literature, nor has it been sufficiently examined empirically.

Therefore, an exploration of the relationship between bicultural competence, stress and coping processes, and academic resilience in Latina/o and Southeast Asian youth appears merited. But first, the empirical evidence relating bicultural competence to academic outcomes will be reviewed to determine whether the former construct is indeed associated with a positive academic trajectory. The next chapter will provide a discussion of stress and coping processes across contexts and cultures within a developmental framework. Lastly, this literature review will conclude with a discussion of the relationship amongst these constructs.

Bicultural Competence and Academic Outcomes

Researchers have long pondered whether biculturalism or bicultural competence is related to other behaviors, specifically, psychological adjustment (see Rotheram-Borus, 1993). Classical theory on biculturalism suggested that the process of adaptation to more than one cultural context was fraught with strife (see Stonequist, 1935). Stonequist argued that conflict arose because acculturating individuals were forced to decide between allegiance with one's own culture or the host's culture. This process was thought to lead to marginality or anomie, a lack of connectivity to either culture. The costs of marginality on psychological health were assumed to be great. Insecurity, anxiety, increased emotionality, distrust, hostility, and defensiveness were believed to be ramifications of this process (also see Goodman, 1964; Lewin, 1948; Mussen, 1953; Paz, 1959).

Current theory has challenged this conceptualization, championing the benefits of biculturalism. A number of researchers and theorists have suggested the following benefits of biculturalism: biocognitive flexibility, knowing and understanding different cultural norms and values, increased options, increased creativity, and adaptability (see

Ramirez, 1984; Ramirez & Casteneda, 1974; Ramirez & Price-Williams, 1974).

However, as previously noted, the relationship between bicultural competence and specific outcomes is inconsistent and inconclusive. For example, Johnston (1972), Kourakis (1983), and Taft (1977) found no relationship between biculturalism and psychological adjustment, whereas Giggs (1977), Greco, Vasta, and Smith (1977), and Wiseman (1971) found negative associations between biculturalism and psychological adjustment (cited in Rotheram-Borus, 1993). These studies are not reviewed herein because the specific focus of this study is on the relationship between bicultural competence and academic resilience, not general adjustment. Following, studies that address this relationship will be reviewed.

Padilla (1994) argues that biculturalism is a very suitable strategy for coping with discriminatory practices in society. He believes that this strategy allows a person to function adequately in the dominant culture while also providing a psychological safety net and retreat where the person can withdraw for refueling from one's family when threatened by racist and discriminatory attitudes. The support received from one's family serves to reaffirm the person's esteem and strengthens connections to the culture of origin. Padilla refers to this phenomenon as the "principle of ethnic protection," and it is through this very phenomenon, Padilla asserts, that biculturalism is maintained across multiple generations.

Further, he distinguishes the motivational processes of biculturalism across multiple generations. For the first-generation, biculturalism is viewed as a must for survival; whereas for the second-generation, it is viewed as an effective means of bridging the culture of origin with that of the dominant culture; for later generations, biculturalism helps to mitigate the effects of racism and discrimination by offering the individual both the support of the group and coping responses that call forth specific ethnic-related social behaviors (Padilla, 1994).

But what about the academic sphere? Is there empirical evidence to support the theory on the positive effects of bicultural competence on academic outcomes? The benefits of bicultural competence on academic functioning have been championed theoretically. For example, Ramirez and Castañeda (1974) have suggested that participation in more than one culture may promote academic success, better psychological adjustment, and greater social flexibility. Buriel et al. (1998) have argued that the cognitive integration and synthesis required for biculturalism may aid students' academic performance. Stanton-Salazar and Dornbusch (1995) argue that bilinguals may have special advantages over working-class, English-dominant students in acquiring the institutional support necessary for school success and social mobility. According to these theorists, bilinguals are believed to retain a significant degree of trust in the school system and in its gatekeepers, whereas working-class, English-dominant students may be acquiring an oppositional stance toward the system. They add that "this kind of bicultural adaptation appears to lead to increases in social capital, both by lowering the risks entailed in help-seeking and by increasing the likelihood of genuine support from institutional agents" (p. 132; see also Stanton-Salazar, 1997).

In the arena of school functioning, the few empirical studies on the effects of bicultural competence on school functioning have produced inconclusive findings regarding this relationship. For example, some studies have found that immigrant students perform as well or better in school than latter-generational and more acculturated students (see Ogbu, 1978; Gibson & Ogbu, 1991; Fuligni, 1997; Kimball, 1968; Nielsen & Fernandez, 1981; Schumaker & Getter, 1977; Vigil & Long, 1981), suggesting that immigrant parents may pass on their high aspirations to their children (Buriel & Cardoza, 1988), whereas second- and third-generation ethnic students are believed to be more sensitive to ongoing patterns of discrimination and prejudice, which in turn may culminate in alienation from school and giving up on education (Gibson and Ogbu, 1991; Ogbu, 1978). These studies appear to suggest that bicultural individuals who embrace both value systems may reveal a positive academic trajectory. However, this construct (i.e., bicultural competence) was not specifically addressed in these studies; thus, the relevance of bicultural competence to the findings is unknown.

However, Gonzalez and Padilla (1998) found that immigrant status alone did not account for a higher GPA, but rather, greater educational performance was contingent on whether students received some form of English or bilingual assistance in the U.S. and whether they received some schooling in Mexico. Again, the findings appear to suggest that biculturalism or bicultural competence may enhance academic functioning; however, as in the previous example, the specific contribution of this construct was not addressed.

What may account for the inconsistency in the findings regarding the impact of biculturalism on psychological and academic adjustment? According to Rotheram-Borus (1993), the following four factors have been found to modify the relationship between biculturalism and other behavioral indices of adjustment: (1) the freedom of contact between the minority and the majority groups; (2) the attitudes of the majority group; (3) the strength of the minority group; and (4) the relationship of the family to the adolescent (also see Rosenthal, 1987). Rotheram-Borus points out that each of these factors highlights the importance of context, and as researchers, it becomes absolutely necessary to assess the context within which data are gathered. For example, socioeconomic (SES) variables (e.g., poverty) repeatedly have been found in the literature to mediate academic outcomes (see the previous section on the theories of the dropout phenomenon). Similarly, discrimination and racism also have been singled out in the literature as possible environmental factors influencing academic outcomes. Therefore, it is absolutely necessary to account or control for contextual factors. The following sections provide a summary of the few studies that have investigated the relationship between bicultural competence and the academic outcomes in Latina/o and Southeast Asian youth.

Latina/O Bicultural Competence and Academic Outcomes

There are a few studies that have linked educational aspirations and achievement among Mexican-American and other minority children to the acculturation process (see Hirano-Nakanishi, 1986). For example, in a study by Buriel, Calzada, and Vasquez (1982), Mexican-American children who remained closely aligned to their traditional culture and values while acculturating, were found to report higher educational aspirations than those who did not. Buenning and Toolefson (1987) found in their sample of Mexican-American children that conflict between ethnic and majority identity was associated with lower academic achievement.

In a recent study by Buriel et al. (1998) of 122 9th- and 10th-grade Latino students from immigrant families who attended a predominantly Latino high school in eastern Los Angeles County in California, a multiple regression analysis showed that academic self-efficacy was the strongest predictor of academic performance, followed by biculturalism and total language brokering (i.e., interpreting for immigrant parents). Biculturalism was measured with the Bicultural Involvement Questionnaire (BIQ) (Szapocznik, Kurtines, & Fernandez, 1980) which assessed the respondent's degree of comfort when speaking English and Spanish independent of each other and their preferred level of involvement in the Euro-American and Latino cultures. Academic performance was measured via self-reported grades.

The researchers note that the relationship between the positive role of biculturalism and academic performance was found even after accounting for the effects of motivational (academic self-efficacy) and linguistic (total language brokering) variables. Buriel et al. (1998) conclude that the greater experience, competence, and comfort in two cultures that biculturalism affords individuals may, in fact, provide bicultural students with more problem-solving strategies, interpersonal skills, and self-confidence for accessing academic resources at school and in their communities. These researchers affirm that bicultural adolescents are better adapted to their dual cultural environment, which serves to minimize the potentially detrimental effects of acculturation (see Rogler, Cortes, & Malgady, 1991; Szapocznik et al., 1980) that may detract from their academic performance. Gandara's (1995) study, discussed above, also supports this conclusion.

However, other studies have not supported such relationships. Suárez-Orozco and Suárez-Orozco (1995) found in their study of 189 adolescents, consisting of 47 Mexican residents, 47 second-generation Mexican Americans, 47 Mexican immigrants, and 47 White Americans, between the ages of 13 and 18 that Mexican resident youths and Mexican immigrants displayed higher achievement motivation than either second-generation Mexican Americans or White Americans. They attributed this loss in achievement press in the second-generation to a combination of multiple factors, such as the stresses of minority status, discrimination, economic hardships, pressure to work, alienating schools, and ambivalence toward authority and schools. Ambivalence toward authority and schools was also cited as an explanatory factor for the diminished achievement motivation of the White Americans. Although this study did not specifically investigate the relationship between bicultural competence and academic achievement, nevertheless it suggests that a bicultural status may not necessarily be protective in terms of academic outcomes to mediate a context of significant psychosocial risk factors.

Another study, which explored the specific role of biculturalism in educational aspirations, also did not provide encouraging support for the beneficial relationship between bicultural competence and academic outcomes. In a study by Der-Karabetian and Ruiz (1997) of a sample of 177 first and second generation, 16 to 19 year old, Mexican-American high school students in Los Angeles, California, a bicultural identity orientation was not associated with higher educational aspirations. These researchers assessed bicultural identity via items that dealt with a sense of belonging, common fate, and sensitivity to praise and insult as both an American (10 items) and a Latino (10 items).

There are a number of interesting observations that may be gleaned from this study. For one, as discussed above, bicultural identity has been distinguished in the literature as a separate construct from bicultural competence; thus, the results may not adequately generalize to other constructs of biculturalism. Furthermore, a bicultural identity orientation has been argued to be a later developing phenomenon (i.e., in adulthood) (see Phinney, 1993); therefore, one may not expect to find any significant associations between this construct and others. In sum, the findings from this study do not significantly add to our understanding of the relationship between bicultural competence and academic resilience and persistence.

In another study, Rotheram-Borus (1989) also found that biculturalism was not related to academic outcomes, in this case, grades. Specifically, she found that biculturalism was not associated with self-esteem, social competence, or grades in integrated school environments. However, she did find that black students who were strongly ethnically identified in this context reported significantly fewer behavior problems, whereas the Hispanic students who were Anglo identified also in this context reported few behavior problems. Moreover, the researcher found that a bicultural reference group orientation was strongly linked to higher social competence but lower grades, and was not related to self-esteem in an integrated school with high cross-ethnic tension.

These results are noteworthy in that they point to the important influence of context on developmental outcomes. For one, in high cross-ethnic tension, integrated school environments, a bicultural orientation may be protective to some degree (i.e., higher social competence), but may not lead to competence across multiple domains (i.e., lower grades). Moreover, based on the findings of this study, biculturalism may not be associated with greater school functioning at least for Hispanics in a context absent of cross-ethnic tension. The results of this study suggest that the impact of biculturalism on outcome appeared to be significantly influenced by context as discussed above.

However, the researcher primarily focused on a bicultural reference group orientation, which according to theorists is an altogether different construct than bicultural competence. In sum, the findings concerning the relationship between bicultural competence and academic functioning are contradictory and inconclusive. Definitive conclusions cannot be made because of the inequivalence of the constructs assessed. Perhaps an investigation of the few studies that also have investigated these constructs but in Southeast Asian youth may shed some light upon this relationship.

Southeast Asian Bicultural Competence and Academic Outcomes

There are far fewer studies that have linked biculturalism or bicultural competence to academic outcomes in Southeast Asian youth. Although not specifically addressing the concept of biculturalism, Fuligni (1997) found that East Asian students from immigrant families revealed greater academic achievement than Latino, Filipino, and European youths (also see Alva, 1993). However, as discussed above the study was seriously hampered by methodological problems (i.e., heterogeneity of the sample).

Further, other studies have not supported such a relationship. For example, in a study by Lese and Robbins (1994) of 39 Cambodian and Vietnamese recent refugees (i.e., date of arrival less than 1 to 9 years) enrolled in a bilingual vocational education program at a high school in a southeastern American city, acculturation was not found to be related to academic achievement. As discussed above acculturation and biculturalism are related but distinct constructs. The former refers to cultural change, whereas the later refers to competence in two cultural systems. The measures they used, however, appear to suggest that the researchers were interested in the relevance of both an Asian and an American cultural orientation or biculturalism in their sample.

They measured acculturation via the Suinn-Lew Asian Self-Identity Acculturation Scale (SL-Asia) (Suinn, Rickard-Figueroa, Lew,

& Vigil, 1987) and an estimate of time in the U.S. The SL-Asia was developed to measure multiple dimensions of acculturation from an Asian perspective (e.g., Asian language familiarity, friendship choice, ethnic identity, cultural behaviors, etc.), whereas the estimate of time in the U.S. has been used to assess a refugee's understanding of American society and culture, and is believed to be associated with the acculturation process (see Matsuoka, 1990; Nicassio, 1985). Academic achievement was assessed via GPA, the Goal Attainment Scaling (GAS) (Kiresuk & Sherman, 1968), and the Work Methods subscale of Survey of Study Habits and Attitudes (Brown & Holtzman, 1967).

As evident, the measures suggest that the researchers were interested in the degree of their subjects' understanding of both cultures. However, the measures were not successful at determining whether the two constructs were related, although they fully expected that acculturation would be related to academic achievement, since the former construct has been found to be related to general adjustment in the literature (see Sokoloff, Carlin, & Pham, 1984). Similarly, others have argued that since American schools favor the cultural values of the majority, students who are not highly acculturated to the mainstream culture are expected to have academic difficulties (cited in Lese & Robbins, 1994). The researchers conclude that participation in the bilingual program may have reduced the role of the acculturation process in academic performance.

Other possible explanations to account for their inability to determine the relationship between these two constructs may be deduced from their methodology. For one, a specific measure of biculturalism or bicultural competence was not utilized. Second, they lacked a specific measure of an understanding of the American culture. Their use of a less than optimal measure (i.e., estimate of time in the U.S.) as an indicator of a refugee's understanding of American society and culture also may have contributed to the inconclusiveness of the study's findings. Third, the researchers utilized a recent refugee sample, and a quarter of the sample were adopted into White families. Consequently, the sample may be currently experiencing acculturative stress or problems with acculturation, which may be a potential confound.

Porte and Torney-Purta (1987) provide some insight into this phenomenon. They found that children placed in foster care with Indochinese families performed better in school and were less depressed than children placed in foster care situations with non-Indochinese families (cited in LaFromboise, Coleman, & Gerton, 1993). Their study provides a possible explanation to account for the inconclusiveness found in Lese and Robbins' (1994) study, and effectively demonstrates the positive impact that maintaining a bicultural environment has on the academic achievement and level of depression among Indochinese youth (LaFromboise, Coleman, & Gerton, 1993). LaFromboise, Coleman, & Gerton (1993) refer to this phenomenon as "groundedness" (see above) or the ability to establish stable social networks in both cultures which, according to these theorists, is an important component of bicultural competence.

Further, speaking a native language at home was found to positively affect Southeast Asian students' educational performance in a study by Blair & Qian (1998), utilizing data from the 1992 National Educational Longitudinal Study (NELS). The maintenance of one's language of origin while acquiring a second language also was noted by LaFromboise, Coleman, & Gerton (1993) as another crucial component of bicultural competence. They referred to this phenomenon as "communication ability" and argue that language competency is a major building block of bicultural competence. Blair & Qian (1998) concluded that native language maintenance is indicative of stronger roots to one's cultural values and that individuals who successfully maintain their native culture while acculturating are more likely to perceive educational advancement as the best means of upward mobility in American society.

A number of models were discussed in an effort to understand how individuals navigate multiple cultural contexts. The alternation model was offered as the superior model to account for biculturalism. Also, bicultural competence was argued to be an effective strategy for acculturating ethnic youth. Further, the role of a number of personal and environmental resources was found in the literature to be associated with bicultural competence.

Although the alternation model and bicultural competence are hypothesized to promote a positive developmental trajectory, the empirical data are inconsistent and inconclusive to this effect. The findings are complicated by a number of methodological problems, such as the use of inferior measures. Further, as noted, the conclusions regarding the study's findings are confounded by the inequivalence of the constructs assessed. More carefully constructed studies are needed to elucidate the relationship between these two constructs, especially across multiple cultural milieus. As previously noted, there is merit in conducting an investigation of the relationship between bicultural competence and academic resilience in Latina/o and Southeast Asian youth. Furthermore, theorists point to the importance of stress and coping processes in this relationship; hence, these constructs also will be discussed and addressed in this study.

CHAPTER 4

Stress, Coping, and Context

> It is said that a significant factor in Latina/o academic achievement is familial support. But sometimes, for whatever reasons, our families of origin are unable to be supportive; yet we persevere, and yes even thrive despite our obstacles. Ultimately, we find that through a relentless faith and love of self we triumph! One discovers that there are multiple paths to resilience.
>
> -anonymous.

Despite their socioeconomic difficulties, a comprehensive literature research revealed few studies conducted on stress and coping processes in Latina/o and Southeast Asian youth. This area of study appears to be in need of further exploration, for it is not clearly reported in the literature how Latinas/os and Southeast Asians are coping with the inherent stressfulness of their academic situation, for example.

Further, it is not clearly understood how diverse sociocultural contexts differentially influence stress and coping processes within these populations, nor is it clear how biculturalism or bicultural competence may influence stress and coping processes to impact academic outcomes. Aldwin (1994a) notes that cultural influences on stress and coping have traditionally been neglected in psychological research. She notes that research interest in stress and coping in particular subcultural groups (e.g., Latina/o and Southeast Asian youth) remains scarce. Empirical studies on such groups are sorely needed to increase our understanding of how bicultural competence affects, for example, stress and coping processes and how these factors combine with situational factors to impact academic outcomes.

53

DEFINITIONS OF STRESS

Mason (1975) identified three definitions of stress. First, stress may refer to a strain. This definition refers to both physiological and emotional reactions of stress. Physiological reactions include peripheral and central nervous system reactions, and neuroendocrine and immune system functions, such as sweaty palms and hyperventilation (Aldwin, 1994a). Emotional reactions to stress generally refer to negative effects, such as anxiety or shame; however, researchers note that stress may be more accurately perceived as having an activating or motivating effect which may be positive or negative depending upon individual and contextual factors (Aldwin, 1994a). For example, a school final (i.e., a stressor) may be perceived positively by one person as a challenge or an opportunity to test one's knowledge, while another person may perceive it as a threat, if not well prepared or confident for the exam.

    Second, stress may be defined as an external event or stressor, such as a major trauma (e.g., war or natural disaster), major life event (e.g., marriage or divorce), noxious environmental characteristic (e.g., pollution or crowding), or as a daily hassle (e.g., commuting) (Aldwin, 1994a). Third, stress may be defined as an experience that arises from a transaction between an individual and her/his environment (Aldwin, 1994a). This perspective takes into consideration perceptions or appraisals of stress (e.g., as a threat or challenge) and the severity of the environmental situation (e.g., major trauma versus daily hassle). Further, it takes into account individual differences in response to environmental demands. From this perspective, individuals are seen to differ in their appraisals or perceptions of stress; in other words, what is stressful for one person may not be stressful for another, as evident in the previous example. Stress may be seen to result from an imbalance between the requirements of the environmental situation and one's perceived ability to cope with it (Aldwin, 1994a).

DEFINITION OF COPING

Coping may be defined as the use of strategies for dealing with actual or anticipated problems and their attendant negative emotions (Aldwin, 1994a). According to White (1974), coping functions in the following three ways: (1) to enable individuals to continue securing adequate information about the environment, (2) to help people maintain satisfactory internal conditions for both action and processing information, and (3) to allow individuals to maintain autonomy or freedom of movement (cited in Aldwin, 1994a).

Coping strategies traditionally have been divided in the literature into three broad categories (see Aldwin, 1994a). Problem-focused coping refers to cognition and behaviors utilized to manage or deal with the stressful situation. Emotion-focused coping refers to strategies utilized to deal with the negative effect elicited by the stressful situation, such as emotional numbing during a crisis situation. Social support coping refers to the utilization of one's social network to deal with a stressful situation. Individuals may seek out their social networks in times of stress for either emotional support (i.e., comforting or nurturance), esteem support (i.e., to feel good about themselves), or to maintain a sense of connectivity or camaraderie with others. Researchers note that individuals are capable of utilizing all three types of coping strategies (i.e., problem-focused coping, emotion-focused coping, and social support coping) in any given stressful situation, but acknowledge that we do have preferred strategies or ways of dealing with stress (see Aldwin, 1994a).

Theoretical Frameworks of Coping

How do theorists and researchers account for individual differences in coping responses? Coping is conceptualized in the literature in the following four ways: (1) person-based approaches posit that personality characteristics are primary in determining how people cope with stress, (2) situation-based approaches posit that the characteristics of different types of stresses "pull for" different types of coping processes, (3) the interactional approach posits that individual and situational characteristics interact to influence coping processes, and (4) the transactional approach posits that coping behavior may change in response to its effects on the situation and that the person, situation, and coping mutually affect each other in a process that evolves over time (Aldwin, 1994a).

Person-based approaches have focused on defense mechanisms, personality traits, and perceptual styles to understand how people cope with stress (see Aldwin, 1994a). The focus of defense mechanisms is to regulate emotions, whereas the focus of personality traits is on the typical ways in which people approach problems based on their personality characteristics. On the other hand, perceptual styles focus on how people process incoming information. A major limitation of person-based theories of coping, however, is that they ignore the diversity of sociocultural contexts and do not acknowledge that different environmental demands may elicit different modes of coping (see Aldwin, 1994a). For example, Aldwin notes that defense mechanisms have very little to do with the actual environmental stimulus of coping but rather have more to do with the person's personality structure which was developed in early childhood. Further, the personality traits perspective assumes that individuals cope consistently with different stressors despite diverse environmental contingencies. Since contextual factors are of interest herein, a strictly person-based theory may not be helpful to understand the phenomena of interest.

The situation-based approach of coping focuses on environmental factors. From this perspective, coping strategies are contingent upon environmental demands. For example, the way a person copes with an exam may be very different from the way that same person deals with the death of a parent. In the former instance, she may utilize a problem-focused strategy to cope with the situation, whereas in the latter, she may use emotion-focused coping to help her deal with the loss. There appears to be ample evidence in the literature to support the view that individuals do respond differently to diverse types of stressors (see Aldwin, 1994a; Mattlin, Wethington, & Kessler, 1990). However, this theory does not help us understand how it is that individuals actively modify their coping strategies to the demands of a particular problem; thus, a strictly situation-based approach similarly may not be helpful in our understanding of the phenomena of interest.

The coping process approach more closely resembles the interactional and transactional approaches previously discussed. This approach considers both the person and the situation, and how both may mutually influence each other. This theory assumes that how an individual copes with a problem is largely dependent upon her/his appraisal of the situation (see Aldwin, 1994a; Lazarus & Folkman, 1984). Appraisals are understood to be a conscious evaluation, based on prior experience, of whether a situation is benign, requiring no coping strategies, or threatening, i.e., involving a harm, loss, or challenge (see Aldwin, 1994a; Lazarus & Folkman, 1984). Another assumption of the model is that individuals are flexible in their choice of coping strategies and actively modify them according to diverse environmental demands (see Aldwin, 1994a; Lazarus & Folkman, 1984). Lastly, individuals are assumed to utilize both problem- and emotion-focused strategies, and that both may be seen as effective means of coping, depending upon the characteristics of the problem (Aldwin, 1994a).

This last approach may be seen as the superior model. Its essential strength lies in the fact that it considers both personal and situational factors of coping. Further, the model appears to account for change. However, there are several major limitations of the model. A limitation of this and the other approaches is the reliance on self-report measures in attempts to capture coping processes (see Aldwin, 1994a). Aldwin notes that with self-report measures, individuals may not be able to report on coping strategies that are unconscious. Further, she notes that individuals' self-reports may be plagued with inaccuracies (see Aldwin, 1994a). Lastly, Aldwin notes that sociocultural influences that also may account for coping differences are typically not explored in these models and in the literature.

THE DEVELOPMENTAL CONTEXT OF STRESS AND COPING

Are there developmental differences in stress and coping processes in adolescence? The literature on stress and coping appears to suggest that there are developmental differences in these processes. For one, adolescents appear to experience unique stressors characteristic of their developmental stage. Compas (1992) differentiated stress into the following three broad categories: generic or normative stress, severe acute stress, and severe chronic stress. According to this researcher, adolescents are exposed to a certain level of generic stress or hassles as an ongoing part of development.

Brown, O'Keeffe, Sanders, and Baker (1986) assessed adolescents' stressors by asking them to spontaneously generate a personal problem (cited in Stark, Spirito, Williams, & Guevremont, 1989). The sample, between the ages of 14 to 18, most frequently cited as their stressors a fear of negative evaluation, fight with/or rejection by friends, fight with/or rejection by the opposite sex, conflict with adults, and concerns regarding the future. However, the researchers did not ask the adolescents to rate the degree of severity of these stressors; therefore it is not known for certain whether these are instances of normative, severe acute, or severe chronic stressors for adolescents.

Similarly, Stark et al. (1989) also found in a representative sample of 14- to 17-year-old adolescents that school, parents, friends, and girl/boyfriends were the most commonly reported problems. These researchers also found interesting gender differences in the order of the most commonly reported problems. For boys, the order of problems was school, parents, friends, and girlfriends; while girls more frequently cited problems with parents, followed by boyfriends, friends, and lastly, school.

These results lend support for the widespread notion that females are more relational than males and thus, are more likely to report relational as opposed to non-relational stressors. Further, the study findings also support the prevalent notion that adolescence is a time when major changes in family, school, and peer group structures occur (see Petersen & Hamburg, 1986). This study, however, focused on the frequencies of reported stressors and not on severity levels; therefore we do not know how these problems are perceived by adolescents.

Wagner and Compas (1990) found that early adolescent girls reported more social, family, peer, intimacy, and social network stressors than boys, and that they perceived these events as more stressful than boys (cited in Compas, Orosan, & Grant, 1993). Thus, it appears that the assessment of the severity levels of reported problems are important in that this type of information may provide us with a deeper understanding of differences (e.g., gender or cultural) in stressors, for example.

In addition to normative stressors, some adolescents may encounter severe, acute events that are of a major or traumatic magnitude. These are not necessarily developmental in nature, but rather, are seen to be situational. A wide range of events fit in this category, including serious injuries, disasters, loss of a loved one through death and parental divorce, etc. Compas, Orosan, and Grant (1993) note that these types of stressors are qualitatively different from normative stress processes in that acute stressors have a discrete onset, affect only a small portion of adolescents, and exert an extreme level of disruption in the adolescents' ongoing world. For an example of this type of stress, the reader is referred to Compas et al.'s (1992) study of adolescents and parental diagnosis of cancer.

Lastly, another subgroup of adolescents may encounter severe, chronic stress as an ongoing part of their environment. Compas et al. (1993) note that this type of stress includes exposure to poverty, neighborhood or familial violence, racism, sexism, and parental psychopathology. Compas et al. (1993) found that this type of stress increases a child or adolescent's risk for a variety of adjustment problems.

This type of stressor may be more salient for some groups such as ethnic minority youth. As previously noted, Latina/o and Southeast Asian youth experience high rates of poverty and racism that may place them at-risk for adjustment problems. Cervantes and Castro (1985) have argued that life events vary in their symbolic properties across cultures such that underrepresented populations may perceive the severity of life events differently than do White populations (cited in Solberg & Villarreal, 1997), and as discussed above, studies have found that the perception of life events also varies by gender (also see Compas, Davis, & Forsythe, 1985). Keefe and Padilla (1987) found the academic experience to be more stressful among Mexican American students than Anglo students (cited in Vazquez & Garcia-Vazquez, 1995). More studies are needed to explore such cross-cultural differences in stressors amongst adolescents.

Some studies, however, point to differences in stressors as a result of immigrant status and acculturation. For example, Sue, Sue, Sue, and Takeuchi (1995) note that immigrants and refugees in the U.S. are exposed to the following stressors: different cultural values, English proficiency problems, minority status including racial/ethnic stereotypes, prejudice, discrimination, and a reduction in available social supports. It appears as if acculturating individuals may be exposed to another level of stressors on top of the normative, developmental and environmental stressors that youth may encounter. Research appears to support this conclusion (see Padilla, 1980; Berry, 1992, 1998; Nicholson, 1997; Sue et al., 1995). However, as previously pointed out in the section on acculturation, these changes may not necessarily imply that the acculturating individual is doomed to a negative developmental trajectory. It may be true that these added stressors may place an individual in an at-risk status, but as previously argued there are a number of resilience factors that may buffer the negative effects of these changes and phenomena.

In sum, Compas et al. note that the three categories of stress are not mutually exclusive. Adolescents may be exposed to one or to all three types of stressors, and a certain type of stressor may contribute to the creation of another type of stressor. For example, the effects of an acute stressor (e.g., divorce) may persist and become a chronic stressor in the adolescent's life (e.g., drop in SES).

The studies reviewed herein highlight the importance of assessing cultural differences in stressors. Most studies of stressors in adolescents have focused on White populations. More studies are needed to determine to what extent stressors differ as a consequence of ethnicity and cultural differences.

Some studies appear to suggest this possibility. For example, a non-refugee study of 70 Southeast Asian adolescents found that Cambodians identified strict discipline by their parents as their greatest stressor, while Hmong and Vietnamese youth identified household chores and academic pressures as their most stressful experiences (Doung Tran, Lee, & Khoi, 1996). Research on Mexican American children and adolescents found that leaving relatives and friends behind when moving, feeling pressured to speak only Spanish at home, living in a home with many people, being ridiculed by other kids when speaking English, being retained, a poor report card, and being sent to the principal were appraised as significant stressors (cited in Alva, 1991). Thus, it appears that stressors do vary across diverse sociocultural contexts. Do coping strategies similarly vary? A discussion of the developmental and cultural differences in coping strategies will follow.

The literature on child and adolescent coping has identified both developmental changes and stabilities in coping. For example, developmental increases in emotion-focused coping have been found in reports of coping with a variety of types of stress (see Altshuler & Ruble, 1989; Band & Weisz, 1988; Compas et al., 1988; Curry & Russ, 1985). On the other hand, no consistent developmental changes have been found in problem-focused coping. Some studies have found no change with age (see Altshuler & Ruble, 1989; Compas et al., 1988; Wertlieb et al., 1987), while others have found a decrease in problem-focused coping with age (see Band & Weisz, 1988; Curry & Russ, 1985).

Worsham, Ey, and Compas (1992) found in their study of the perceptions of control and coping in children, adolescents, and young adults whose parents have cancer that appraisals of control did not change with age; however, the use of emotion-focused and dual-focused coping (i.e., strategies that accomplish both problem- and emotion-focused coping functions) increased from childhood to adolescence but not between adolescence and young adulthood (cited in Compas, Orosan, & Grant, 1993). These findings add to previous studies that found developmental increases in emotion-focused coping and stability in problem-focused coping from childhood to adolescence. However, the developmental differences in social support coping were not investigated in this study.

Research suggests that social support may be an important coping strategy in the academic domain for ethnically diverse youth. For example, Hernandez (1993) found in his qualitative interview study of 80 Mexican American high school youth in Pueblo, Colorado, that teacher support, peer instrumental support, and parent motivational support significantly contributed to academic achievement among students identified as resilient. Gonzalez and Padilla (1997) also found that family and peer support were consistent predictors of academic resilience in their sample of 2,169 Mexican American students in three California high schools (also see Alva, 1991; Arellano & Padilla, 1996; Gandara, 1995; Hernandez, 1993; Stanton-Salazar, 1998).

Stark, Spirito, Williams, and Guevremont (1989) investigated the use of emotion-focused and social support coping in their adolescent sample. These coping strategies were found to differ by gender. Female adolescents reported using social support more frequently than males, whereas male adolescents reported using wishful thinking (i.e., emotion-focused coping) more often than females and perceived resignation (i.e., emotion-focused coping) as more effective than did females. Compas, Malcarne, and Fondacaro (1988) found in their study of adolescent coping that girls used more emotion-focused strategies than did boys in response to academic events. These results are consistent with studies on adults that have found more frequent use of emotion-focused and social support coping strategies for females (see Billings & Moos, 1981; Stone & Neale, 1984).

Thus, it appears that emotion-focused, problem-focused, and social support coping are salient coping strategies for adolescents. Although social support coping in Latina/o youth has been studied fairly extensively (also see Leyva, 1990; Salgado de Snyder, 1987; Solberg, Valdez, & Villareal, 1994), research on emotion- and problem-focused coping in Latina/o youth has not been investigated as comprehensively. This research's focus on social support coping in this population may be an artifact of the belief that Latinas/os are highly familialistic and collectivistic (see Marin & Marin Van Oss, 1991). However, a study of Puerto Rican college students found that active coping (i.e., problem-focused coping) predicted low levels of psychological symptomatology and high academic performance (cited in Zea, Jarama, & Bianchi,

1995). Mena, Padilla, and Maldonado (1987) and Vazquez and Garcia-Vazquez (1995) and also found that Mexican American and multicultural students frequently used active-type coping.

Furthermore, based on a comprehensive literature search, virtually no developmental studies have been conducted on non-refugee Southeast Asian stress and coping processes. Refugee Southeast Asians are a special population who are believed to be exposed to unique stressors that may significantly impact adjustment (see Ahearn & Athey, 1991; Al-Issa & Tousignant, 1997; Bromley, 1988; Kinzie, 1993; Nicassio, Solomon, Guest, McCullough, 1986; Nicholson, 1997; Sue, Sue, sue, & Takeuchi, 1995; Ying, Akutsu, Zhang, & Huang, 1997).

Thus, it appears that there are some interesting cross-cultural differences regarding coping processes (e.g., relational issues appraised less stressful). However, we cannot conclude this with certainty because of the dearth in cross-cultural studies of stress and coping processes. More cross-cultural developmental studies are needed to determine whether there are differences in these processes across these populations.

Interestingly, the developmental literature suggests that coping strategies vary depending upon the characteristics of the reported problem. This phenomenon has been noted across the lifespan. Researchers and theorists conceptualize that flexibility in the way a person copes with different stressors is a hallmark of effective adaptation (see Cohen, 1984; Lazarus & Folkman, 1984; Meichenbaum, 1985; Moos & Billings, 1982). Flexibility is characterized by changing the coping strategies one uses in response to the demands of different stressors and/or in response to the same stressor as demands change over the course of a stressful encounter, whereas high levels of consistency across different stressful episodes and over reliance on certain strategies are characteristics supposedly associated with maladaptive responses to stress (Compas, Forsythe, & Wagner, 1988).

Studies appear to support the perspective that coping strategies vary as a function of the problem. For example, adolescents in Stark et al.'s study utilized a wider variety of coping strategies with an increased frequency when attempting to deal with male-female relationship problems as opposed to school or parental problems. Adolescents appeared to engage in more concerted efforts when dealing with intimacy problems. Compas et al. (1988) also found evidence that adolescents perceived the causes of academic stressors as more controllable than the causes of social stressors and generated more problem-focused alternatives for coping with academic stress. The findings suggest that the situation itself appears to pull for specific types of coping and that individuals appear to match their coping efforts with appraisals of control (also see Folkman & Lazarus, 1980). However, other studies have found that attributions and coping processes are characterized by high levels of consistency in adolescents and adults (see Stone & Neale, 1984; Wills, 1986). These inconsistencies in the literature prevent us from arriving at a firm conclusion regarding the malleability of coping processes. Further, there are relatively few studies, which have investigated this phenomenon in culturally diverse groups, which further compromises our understanding of this process.

However, Aldwin (1994a) has argued that bicultural individuals may develop two separate coping repertoires in some situations. This phenomenon was observed in a Nissei, second-generation Japanese-American sample by Kiefer (1974) and in a sample of Aboriginal adolescents in Australia by Davidson, Nurcombe, Kearney, and Davis (1978). Bicultural individuals in these samples appeared to be utilizing different coping strategies depending upon whether the difficulty involved group members or individuals outside their cultural group.

In sum, it appears as if there are developmental differences in coping processes. Normative stressors of youth appear to revolve around issues of intimacy for some. Further, significant gender differences for some groups are evident in the empirical data on adolescent coping. Some studies suggest that females appear to be more concerned about relational issues and tend to utilize more emotion-focused and social support coping than adolescent males. The findings are significant because the literature appears to suggest that these coping strategies are associated with both positive and negative consequences (see Compas, 1987). These studies appear to suggest that females may be more vulnerable than males to certain types of stressors. Furthermore, studies of the situational context of coping processes in adolescence have produced inconsistent results. Some studies suggest that coping is consistent under similar circumstances but vary as features of the problem, environment, or cognitive appraisals of the environment change, while other studies find consistency in coping across a wide variety of stressful situations

(Compas, 1987). However, studies vary in their methodology; thus, complicating comparability of the research findings. Lastly, relatively few studies have been undertaken on ethnic minority youth; therefore our understanding of cultural differences in stress and coping processes remains, at best, vague. Contextual and cultural factors of coping will be investigated in the following sections.

BICULTURAL COMPETENCE, STRESS AND COPING PROCESSES ACROSS CONTEXTS, AND ACADEMIC OUTCOMES

In the previous section, several theoretical frameworks of stress and coping processes were discussed. In this section, a discussion of how bicultural competence may affect coping will be explored by first discussing the ways in which the cultural context may impact this process. The coping process framework will be utilized to guide the discussion of coping due to the relevance of this theory for the study. Lastly, a discussion of how the two phenomena, bicultural competence and coping processes, may influence academic outcomes will be undertaken.

According to Aldwin (1994a), culture affects the stress and coping processes in the following four ways:

> First, the cultural context shapes the types of stressors that an individual is likely to experience. Second, culture may also affect the appraisal of the stressfulness of a given event. Third, cultures affect the choice of coping strategies that an individual utilizes in any given situation. Finally, culture provides different institutional mechanisms by which an individual can cope with stress (p. 193).

Aldwin depicts this process in her sociocultural model of stress, coping, and adaptation (see Aldwin, 1994a). The model, however, depicts a singular cultural beliefs and values pool, which influences coping processes. For bicultural individuals (e.g., Latina/o and Southeast Asians in the U.S.), two cultural pools are relevant since such individuals draw their resources, values, beliefs, etc. from both their ethnic group and the dominant group (see the section on biculturalism).

Based on the theoretical model but from a dual-cultural perspective, the bicultural context is believed to shape the types of stressors an individual will experience. A bicultural individual may encounter stressors that are specific to each sociocultural context. For example, a Latina/o or Southeast Asian youth may experience racism in the sociocultural context of school, whereas in the context of home or one's ethnic enclave, such an experience may be unusual.

Also, according to the theory, the cultural context is believed to affect the appraisal process. For example, academic challenges (e.g., exams) may be appraised positively for some immigrant groups; however, for some non-immigrant ethnic groups, the same challenges may be perceived rather negatively (i.e., as a threat). There appears to be some evidence to support this conclusion (see Fuligni, 1997). Researchers hypothesize that these differences may be attributable to the greater adherence of immigrant populations to traditional values that emphasize achievement. Moreover, these values are believed to atrophy over subsequent generations due to acculturation and the ramifications of societal inequality (e.g., discrimination) (see the previous section on theories of the dropout phenomenon). However, bicultural individuals are believed to straddle both their traditional value system and the dominant cultural value system; therefore they are believed to not experience the loss of achievement motivation, for example (see the section on bicultural competence). Further, biculturals are believed to appraise both cultural contexts favorably, which may facilitate their ability to integrate the two systems with obvious benefits (see LaFromboise, Coleman, & Gerton, 1993).

Further, culture is believed to affect the choice of coping strategies that an individual utilizes. For example, some forms of social support may be perceived rather negatively by one's cultural group, while others may be viewed more favorably. It has been noted in the literature that some cultural groups, such as Southeast Asians, discourage the use of outside professionals (e.g., therapists) for personal and familial psychosocial problems (see Chao, 1992; Huang, 1998; Nishio & Bilmes, 1998). Instead, such cultural groups may be encouraged to utilize family members, friends, or community members to help them deal with their problems. According to the theory discussed above on biculturalism, a bicultural individual may manifest behavioral flexibility in such a situation. She or he may be able to access both forms of social support, flexibly and adaptively, depending upon the demands of the problem, which may culminate in a substantial increase in one's repertoire of coping strategies. The flexible and adaptive use of coping strategies is another essential component of the coping process approach discussed above.

Lastly, culture is believed to provide an individual with different institutional mechanisms to cope with stress. An illustration of this phenomenon may be gleaned from the previous example. For some cultural groups, community mental health facilities may be an optimal recourse for psychosocial difficulties; however, for other cultures such an option may be culturally dissonant. A further example may be found in the use of faith healers or *curanderas/os* in some indigenous cultures. This form of holistic healing is currently enjoying renewed enthusiasm in some communities (e.g., Mexican and Puerto Rican) (see Ramirez, 1998). Bicultural individuals may benefit greatly via the ability to access institutional mechanisms from both their traditional and the dominant culture and thereby increase their repertoire of coping strategies. Again this illustrates the notion of the flexibility and adaptiveness of bicultural individuals.

In sum, coping efforts are affected by the following six factors: (1) social support from both the traditional and dominant cultural groups, (2) reactions of others in the situation across the two cultural contexts, (3) individual bicultural coping resources, (4) appraisals of stress across the two cultural milieus, (5) individual bicultural values and beliefs, and (6) the resources and demands provided by the two cultural groups.

So how may the two phenomena, bicultural competence and coping processes, influence academic outcome? According to Aldwin (1994a) coping outcomes are believed to have cultural, social, situational, psychological, and physiological effects. Bridging bicultural competence, coping processes with academic outcomes, biculturals may actively modify or create bicultural institutions (e.g., school based ethnic clubs) that reward their academic competencies, for example, and further benefit them through the augmentation of their social support networks. Empirical evidence appears to suggest that peers do influence academic performance (see the section above on academic outcomes). For example, Fuligni (1997) found in his sample of high achieving Asian American immigrants that friends were instrumental in encouraging and supporting each other in their academic endeavors.

Furthermore, Aldwin (1994a) notes that the relation between culture and individual coping is not unidirectional, but rather bidirectional. Not only is the bicultural context capable of influencing changes in individual patterns of coping (i.e., increasing coping repertoires), but the individual also is capable of changing existing culturally prescribed patterns of coping in the process of integration, as evident in the previous discussion. This perspective of coping emphasizes that coping behavior nearly always occurs in a sociocultural context and is both affected by that context and contributes to its change (Aldwin, 1994a; Gross, 1970).

There are several other models in the acculturation literature that may be helpful in our understanding of the complex relationship amongst these phenomena. For example, Berry (1998) offers the following model of the process of acculturation and adaptation (see figure 4.1).

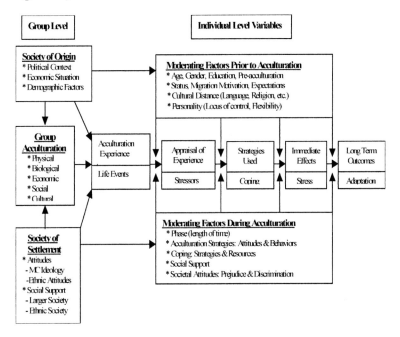

Figure 4.1. Acculturation and adaptation framework. Source: Berry (1992).

The model depicts group or cultural level phenomena on the left. These phenomena are mainly situational factors, such as the political context of the society of origin, the society of settlement's attitudes towards immigrant groups, and its multicultural (MC) ideology. Individual or psychological-level factors are illustrated on the right side of the model. The large top box features phenomena that may exist prior to acculturation, while the large bottom box illustrates those factors that may arise during the process of acculturation. The middle of the framework depicts the main cultural and psychological acculturation phenomena, which flow from left to right.

This process is believed to begin with contact between the two cultural groups initiated by the process of immigration, for example. These cultural group factors may be viewed as either resources or stressors by the acculturating group. For example, some settlement communities may be more tolerant of ethnic diversity than others or may provide more resources (e.g., social support) for refugees or immigrant populations, which may facilitate the acculturation process. This process of culture contact is thought to bring about multiple changes for the acculturating group (e.g., the family unit) in its attempts to reconcile diverse cultural milieus; these changes then affect the individual who is experiencing acculturation.

Acculturating individuals appear to be influenced by both the society of origin and the society of settlement, as well as by their group's (e.g., the family unit) cultural changes in adaptation to a different cultural context. Based on the literature review on biculturalism, bicultural individuals appear to be more effective at integrating these diverse changes and phenomena than those who adopt other strategies (e.g., the marginal strategy). As argued above, biculturalism appears to be the superior strategy to adopt in the process of acculturation.

Further, the model stipulates that the acculturating individual may experience a number of psychological phenomena and changes. Based on the model, life events appear to be important influences on an individual's acculturation experience. From a bicultural perspective, individuals who are able to appraise both cultural systems positively may have derived more positive life experiences throughout the process of acculturation; consequently, they may be more likely to experience a favorable acculturation trajectory, such as the development of bicultural competence (see the section above on bicultural competence).

Furthermore, the acculturation experience, in this case biculturalism, is seen to influence appraisals of stressors as discussed above, affecting the choice of strategies one may utilize in coping with the difficulty. As argued above, bicultural individuals may have a greater repertoire of coping strategies at their disposal because they are able to draw resources from two cultural systems. Coping efforts are seen in the model to have immediate effects on stress, modulating (i.e., increasing or decreasing) levels of stress, depending upon the coping strategy utilized, which then finally leads to the individual's adaptation. For this study, the final outcome is academic resilience and persistence. Moreover, the moderating factors, pre- and during acculturation, are seen to provide the broad structure in which acculturation takes place (see Berry, 1992; 1998).

A strength of the model is that it combines both structural and process features (Berry, 1998). Berry notes that this process evolves over time and has been found to be highly variable depending on the nature of a person's psychological acculturation. Further, Berry notes that eventual adaptation also has been found to depend on specific features of group-level factors and on the moderating influence of individual factors that exist prior to or arise during acculturation. Berry's model nicely complements Aldwin's theory of culture's influence on the stress and coping process. In conjunction, both theoretical frameworks greatly enhance our understanding of the phenomena of inquiry.

In the subsequent chapter, the study's guiding theoretical model will be presented and discussed. It synthesizes aspects of both of these models. In the following section, a review of the few studies that have investigated the relationships among bicultural competence, stress and coping processes, and academic outcomes will be undertaken.

REVIEW OF THE EMPIRICAL EVIDENCE

No studies have been located across cultures that have attempted to link bicultural competence to coping processes and academic outcomes. Berry (1998) notes that no single study has incorporated or verified all aspects of his framework. Further, he points out that his model is a composite, assembling concepts and findings from numerous smaller-scale studies. Therefore, the studies that I will review herein cannot provide us with a comprehensive understanding of the relationship amongst these constructs. At best, they provide us with an inkling of this complex process.

As aforementioned, there appears to be evidence to link bicultural competence to academic resilience and persistence, but the empirical evidence of the moderating role of stress and coping processes in this relationship remains unclear. Theories reviewed herein appear to suggest that bicultural competence is related to stress and coping processes; however, empirical studies have not been conducted to flesh-out this relationship. Further, the literature reviewed in this chapter also appears to suggest that stress and coping processes are related to academic outcomes; however, this information does not aid in our comprehension of the moderating role of these processes, nor does it provide us with an understanding of the possible antecedents in this complex relationship.

Theory appears to suggest that stress and coping processes do moderate outcomes. For example, Holahan and Moos (1991; 1994) have proposed a resources model of coping where personal and social resources are related to subsequent mental health both directly and indirectly, through adaptive coping responses (cited in Holahan, Valentiner, & Moos, 1995). Similarly, Lazarus and Folkman (1984) have defined resources, such as social support, as what an individual "draws on in order to cope" and have argued that such resources "precede and influence coping" (cited in Holahan et al., 1995).

Support for the relevance of this model to adolescents comes from several recent empirical studies. Holahan et al. (1995) found in their study of 241 eighteen-year-old college freshmen that parental support was associated with better psychological adjustment both directly and indirectly, through adaptive coping responses (i.e., approach coping). Similar results also have been found for Hispanic adolescents, indicating that this phenomenon may be relevant for diverse groups. Craen (1994) found that among his sample of 300 inner-city Hispanic adolescents between the ages of 11- and 15-years, social support from parents, teachers, and friends related to psychological adjustment both directly and indirectly, through adaptive coping strategies. Holahan et al. (1995) surmise that the paths vary as a function of the level of stressors adolescents face, with the indirect path through coping being stronger under increased adaptive demands.

Similarly, Vega, Hough, and Miranda (1985) have proposed a diathesis-stress model but for college adjustment. These theorists assert that social support is both directly related to college adjustment and moderates the relationship between stress and adjustment. From this perspective, a person who perceives social support as available will indicate better academic adjustment than one who does not perceive this resource. This model appears to focus on the appraisal process rather than on coping effort, per se. Subjective appraisals of stressful events in school and social environment have been found to be important mediators of academic achievement (cited in Alva, 1991). Further, stress has been found in the literature to be associated with academic adjustment and that experiencing more than twelve stressful life events may be associated with negative academic performance (cited in Solberg & Villareal, 1997). Moreover, the literature strongly suggests that the appraisal given to potentially stressful events determines the subsequent coping responses and behaviors of individuals who are exposed to stress (Compas, 1987).

In this chapter, the developmental literature on stress and coping processes was reviewed. Most empirical studies of these processes have focused on European American populations; thus, our understanding of these phenomena in ethnically and culturally diverse groups is at best crude. The few studies reviewed herein suggest that stress and coping processes do vary depending upon developmental, contextual, and cultural factors. In sum, the study findings highlight the importance of assessing coping responses across developmental stages, contexts, and cultures.

According to Aldwin (1994a), a situational determinant approach to the conceptualization of coping argues that the types of strategies that individuals use to cope with problems depend highly on environmental demands or the characteristics of different types of stresses. But as evident in the discussion above, coping strategies differ developmentally as well. Further, Aldwin notes that stressors vary in characteristics and in the different types of solutions and coping processes that are elicited. As argued above, stressors also appear to vary developmentally, ethnically, and by gender.

Lastly, diverse models also were reviewed in an attempt to understand the complex relationship amongst bicultural competence, stress and coping processes across contexts, and academic resilience. In summation, the models appear to support the notion that bicultural competence may predict academic resilience and persistence via decreased appraisals of stress and enhanced coping efforts. However, the empirical evidence substantiating and explicating this relationship is nonexistent. Therefore the study will attempt to flesh-out these relationships across cultures (i.e., Latina/o and Southeast Asian) and contexts (i.e., familial and academic). In the following chapter, a model will be proposed for this purpose, and alternative and exploratory models will be introduced.

CHAPTER 5

Cross Cultural Research

DESIGN

A cross-cultural research design was chosen for the following reasons. Cross-cultural research, herein defined as "the explicit, systematic comparison of psychological variables under different cultural conditions in order to specify the antecedents and processes that mediate the emergence of behavior differences" (Eckensberger, 1972) (p. 100), is believed to be an effective means of determining the antecedents and mediators of phenomena (Berry, 1980). Since the study explored both indirect and direct effects models, this design was considered appropriate. Further, Berry notes that this type of research is devoted to a search for cause and effect relationships or covariation between two levels of variables – the cultural and the behavioral. This study explored the relationship between cultural level variables (i.e., ethnicity) and individual level variables (e.g., bicultural competence and coping). Triandis, Malpass, and Davidson (1972) asserted that by comparing two cultural groups, utilizing equivalent methods of measurement, we may be more effective at disentangling cultural from behavioral variables of a given phenomenon.

Further, for a truly legitimate comparative analysis, the phenomena of study must be comparable across cultures. Berry (1980) notes that "to compare two phenomena, they must share some feature in common and to compare them to some advantage, they should usually differ on some feature" (p. 8). A common underlying process, thought to underlie academic resilience for the groups of study, may be socioeconomic status (see Chapter 2). Education is thought to be a significant means of upward mobility, especially for socially and economically disadvantaged minority groups (see Smith, 1995). Academic resilience may be an effective strategy for some Latinas/os and Southeast Asian youth to improve their socioeconomic status. In this way, academic resilience may be seen to be functionally equivalent across these groups, as a means of upward mobility. In elaborating on functional equivalence, Berry (1969) notes:

> Thus, functional equivalence of behavior exists when the behavior in question has developed in response to a problem shared by two or more social/cultural groups, even though the behavior in one society does not appear to be related to its counterpart in another society. These functional equivalences must pre-exist as naturally occurring phenomena; they are discovered and cannot be created or manipulated by the cross-cultural psychologist. Without this equivalence, it is suggested, no valid cross-cultural behavioral comparisons may be made (p. 122).

Yet for a worthwhile comparison, the phenomena must be sufficiently different across these groups; this information we do not know for certain because of the aforementioned methodological constraints and lack of studies investigating the phenomena of interest across the two groups (i.e., Latina/o and Southeast Asian). Thus, it appears that there may be functional equivalence in the phenomena under investigation. However, whether and to what degree the phenomena differ across the groups is not clearly explicated in the literature.

MODEL

The purpose of the between-group comparisons (testing the primary hypotheses) in this study was to address differences between Latina/o and Southeast Asian adolescents in (1) bicultural competence, (2) stress and coping processes across contexts, and (3) academic resilience. Additionally, several exploratory variables were investigated herein, which also were thought to impact GPA; these are (1) self-esteem, (2) depressed mood, (3) academic goals, (4) perceived parental warmth, and (5) perceived school discrimination. Group differences for these indices also were explored. The secondary (within-group) hypotheses related to (a) within-group associations among the above indices and to (b) the identification of the model with the strongest relationship to academic resilience.

As discussed in Chapters 2, 3, and 4, bicultural competence appears to be associated with academic resilience; further, stress and coping processes may moderate this relationship. Theoretically, these relationships receive some support in the literature; however, the empirical evidence to support this conclusion is virtually non-existent. This study is an attempt to remedy this dearth in the literature. Further, it is understood that there may be other factors that significantly impact GPA; hence, an exploration of some of these factors (i.e., self-esteem, depressed mood, academic goals, perceived parental warmth, and perceived school discrimination) also was undertaken.

Figure 4.1 depicts a model to understand the complexity of these relationships (see Chapter 4). Specifically, it describes a model of the relationships among acculturation, various mediating factors both prior and during acculturation, stress and coping processes, and adaptive outcomes. Separate models were not proposed for the Latina/o and Southeast Asian participants for the following reasons. First, this process is believed to apply cross-culturally, although progression through the stages is viewed to be highly variable depending upon a person's psychological acculturation (see Berry, 1998). Second, there was insufficient power to conduct a separate structural equation model for the Southeast Asian group ($\underline{n}$ = 89). Third, separate correlation matrices were generated for each ethnic group; however, these matrices did not differ significantly (see Chapter 7).

Herein an indirect/direct effects model (see Figure 5-1 below), which is a partial test of Berry's (1992) model (see Figure 4-1 in Chapter 4), was explored. The working model of the study explored only individual-level phenomena, however. Also, the model specifically focused on bicultural competence, rather than on the global construct of acculturation and on academic resilience instead of the generic construct of adaptive outcomes.

At the far left of the model, the acculturation strategy of biculturalism, specifically, self-reported bicultural competence is presented (see Figure 5.1 below). According to the theory, the development of bicultural competence is contingent upon the integration of various life experiences or events across cultures (e.g., knowledge of cultural values of both the second culture and the culture of origin) (see LaFromboise, Coleman, & Gerton, 1993).

In the center of the model, stress and coping processes are depicted across two sociocultural contexts: the familial and the academic (see Figure 5.1 below). The familial context is believed to reflect and support the values of collectivism and familialism, which have been found to be important cultural values for Latinas/os (see Marin & Marin Van Oss, 1991) and Southeast Asians (see Huang, 1998); in contrast, the academic context is believed to promote individualism (see Triandis, 1995). Bicultural Latinas/os and Southeast Asians are believed to embrace both collectivism and individualism (see LaFromboise, Coleman, & Gerton, 1993; Triandis, 1995). According to LaFromboise et al. (1993), bicultural individuals are believed to appraise both cultural contexts and therefore culturally specific stressors positively, as less stressful and as challenges as opposed to threats, for example. A cross-cultural, positive appraisal process is believed by these researchers to facilitate the integration of these two cultural systems and therefore promote the development of bicultural competence. Thus, the sample is expected to appraise both the familial and the academic situations favorably, as less stressful and as challenges.

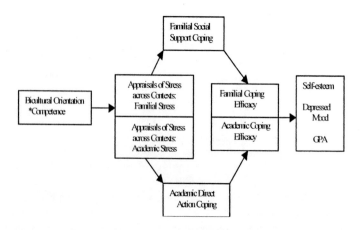

Figure 5-1: Cross-cultural, bicultural competence and academic resilience model

According to the theories of biculturalism and culture's influence on stress and coping processes, some bicultural individuals may utilize different coping efforts depending upon the characteristics of their sociocultural contexts (see Aldwin, 1994a). Hence, a familial stressor conceivably may pull for more social support coping because this situation reflects the value of collectivism. Collectivist cultures have been noted to emphasize reciprocity and mutual support (see Marin & Marin Van Oss, 1991; Triandis, 1995). Similarly, an academic stressor conceivably may pull for more direct action coping because this situation reflects the value of individualism. Individualist cultures have been noted to emphasize self-enhancement and individual problem solving (see Marin & Marin Van Oss, 1991; Triandis, 1995). Therefore it is expected that biculturally competent individuals of the sample will reveal social support coping in the familial situation and direct action coping in the academic context. However, the findings from the studies reviewed in Chapter 4 have provided inconsistent and inconclusive support for these relationships. Hence, these relationships are worthy of more systematic and comprehensive investigations.

According to the model, coping efforts are believed to have immediate effects on stress by either increasing or decreasing stress levels. For bicultural individuals, social support coping in the familial situation and direct action coping in the academic context are expected to decrease stress levels. Further, this adaptive behavioral flexibility is expected to promote coping efficacy across contexts for the sample. Ultimately, these adaptive processes are expected to promote self-esteem, decrease depressed mood, and enhance academic resilience in the sample.

The model also explored the possibility that bicultural competence may have a direct rather than an indirect effect on academic resilience (see Figure 5.1 above). The research and theory discussed in Chapter 3 appears to suggest that there may be a relationship between bicultural competence and academic resilience; however, it is unclear in the literature whether the former construct has a direct or an indirect effect on the latter construct. For this reason, a direct effects path also was explored in the model. Specifically, the model posited that bicultural competence also might have a direct effect on academic resilience.

Regarding the exploratory variables and relationships, as aforementioned some of the exploratory variables were utilized in this model to explore whether bicultural competence is related to other adaptive processes (i.e., self-esteem and decreased depressed mood) besides academic resilience. Lastly, two alternative study models and one exploratory model were generated in Chapter 7 to determine whether these models provided a better explanation of the research findings than the original study model. The alternative study models sought to determine whether utilizing different configurations of the variables of interest provided a better explanation of the study findings than the original study model. Separate models were generated for each context (i.e., familial and academic). The exploratory model sought to determine the relationship of environmental factors (i.e., perceived parental warmth and perceived school discrimination) with academic resilience.

Environmental factors have been argued to be important influences for adolescent behavior and development (see Bronfenbrenner, 1979; 1986; Compas & Wagner, 1991). Indeed, environmental or ecological factors, such as parental stress and parental marital conflict, have been found in the literature to be important influences for adolescent psychological adjustment. For example, many studies have found that children of stressed parents (e.g., separation or divorce) are at-risk for a wide spectrum of adjustment problems, including poor academic performance, difficulties with peers, higher levels of antisocial behavior, and symptoms of psychopathology (Burbach & Borduin, 1986; Downey & Coyne, 1990; Ge, Conger, Lorenz, Shanahan, & Elder, 1995).

Further, adolescents from authoritarian households that were low on warmth and support, emphasizing conformity and obedience, performed poorly on verbal and math achievement tests (see Baumrind, 1989). Furthermore, adolescent girls were affected more adversely by authoritarian upbringing than adolescent boys in that they revealed greater internalizing problem behavior and were not self-regulated, socially responsible, cognitively motivated, resilient, or optimistic (Baumrind, 1989). Therefore the role of perceptions of parental warmth in academic resilience merits further investigation.

Other ecological factors that contribute to school performance were discussed in Chapter 2 in the section of theories of the dropout phenomenon. The institutional culture conflict theory, summarized by Ianni and Orr (1996), places the onus of the dropout problem on the school environment. This theory describes dropping out as the result of cultural dissonance between the school culture and the culture of the student. From this perspective, the student body and professional culture of a school (e.g., teachers and staff), "may be dissonant for some students, undercutting the sense of community and inclusiveness for these students and discouraging their continued school attendance" (p. 300-01). School discrimination has been argued to be culturally dissonant for youth, impacting academic outcomes significantly (see Chapter 2); therefore, the role of perceptions of school discrimination in academic resilience also merits further investigation.

In sum, since environmental factors have been noted in the literature to significantly influence academic outcomes, it was deemed important to explore the relationships among some of these variables (i.e., perceived parental warmth and perceived school discrimination) with academic resilience in an exploratory model. A guiding model was proposed herein, which attempted to integrate cultural factors (i.e., ethnicity) with individual variables (e.g., bicultural competence and coping) and adaptive processes (e.g., self-esteem and academic resilience). Some of the exploratory variables were incorporated into this model and into later alternative study models; others were utilized later to generate an exploratory model (see results section in Chapter 7).

Between-Group Comparisons

No studies have been located that have compared Latina/o to Southeast Asian youth specifically on bicultural competence. Although theoretically, the process of acculturation is believed to be similar across cultures (see Berry, 1992; 1998), no empirical studies have systematically explored whether bicultural competence differs across the cultures of interest. Therefore it is not known for certain how the two groups will compare; thus, the null hypothesis of equivalence will be supported herein. In other words, Latina/o and Southeast Asian adolescents are hypothesized to not differ in bicultural competence.

Similarly, no empirical studies have been conducted which have compared Latina/o to Southeast Asian adolescents on stress and coping processes across contexts. Theoretically, stress and coping processes are believed to be different across diverse sociocultural groups and contexts (see Chapter 4). Although the literature appears to suggest that both groups experience similar types of stressors (e.g., socioeconomic and acculturation) (see Chapters 2 and 4), no empirical studies have been found that compared Latina/o to Southeast Asian youth specifically on stress and coping processes across multiple sociocultural contexts. Therefore it also is not known for certain how the two groups will compare; thus, the null hypothesis of equivalence similarly will be supported herein. To put it simply, Latina/o and Southeast Asian youth are hypothesized to not differ in stress and coping processes across diverse sociocultural contexts.

On the other hand, empirical studies appear to suggest that Asian Americans as a group out-perform Latinas/os on multiple indices of academic performance (see Chapter 2). However, as pointed out in the literature review in Chapter 2, the empirical studies that have explored this phenomenon are critically flawed in that they assume that Asian Americans are a homogenous group. As pointed out, the various subgroups that comprise this supracategory, are distinct socioeconomically and academically. Similarly, it was pointed out in Chapter 2 that the various Latina/o subgroups also are not homogenous. Therefore it also is not known for certain how Latinas/os and Southeast Asians from this sample will compare; thus, the null hypothesis of equivalence similarly will be supported herein. In other words, Latina/o and Southeast Asian youth are hypothesized to not differ in academic resilience.

Academic resilience also may be influenced by a number of other variables, some of which were incorporated in the original study model and in the alternative study models, while others were incorporated in the exploratory models. The variables include self-esteem, depressed mood, academic goals, perceived parental warmth, and perceived school discrimination. It is not known for certain how the two groups will compare on these exploratory variables; thus, the null hypothesis of equivalence similarly will be supported herein. To put it simply, Latina/o and Southeast Asian youth are hypothesized to not differ in self-esteem, depressed mood, academic goals, perceived parental warmth, and perceived school discrimination.

Within-Group Patterns

According to the model, the predicted relationship between bicultural competence and stress and coping processes theoretically do not differ for the Latina/o and Southeast Asian groups (see Berry, 1992; 1998). The relationship between acculturation and adaptive processes is believed to be similar across cultures. However, no studies have been conducted to determine whether this relationship is substantiated empirically across the groups of interest. Because of the theoretical model, it is hypothesized that bicultural competence is related to lower stress ratings and greater likelihood of appraising stress as a challenge across domains, which in turn is related to greater social support coping in the familial context and greater direct action coping in the academic context. Further, these coping responses are hypothesized to be related to greater coping efficacy across contexts.

According to the model, the predicted relationships amongst stress and coping processes across diverse sociocultural contexts theoretically do not differ for the Latina/o and Southeast Asian groups (see Berry, 1992; 1998). Although other theorists and researchers point out that this process is indeed variable cross-culturally and cross-situationally (see Aldwin, 1994a), empirical studies that have investigated this phenomenon in Latina/o and Southeast Asian youth are non-existent (see Chapter 4). Further, according to the model, stress and coping processes across contexts theoretically are predicted to be related to adaptive processes (e.g., self-esteem) and academic resilience (see Chapter 4). However, the empirical evidence also does not exist to either refute or support these relationships across the groups of interest. Because of the theoretical model, it is hypothesized that coping efficacy, cross-situationally, is related to greater self-esteem, lower depressed mood, and greater academic resilience.

Although theoretically this relationship is supported (see Berry, 1992; 1998), no one has systematically examined how bicultural competence relates to stress and coping processes across contexts and academic resilience across the groups of interest. According to the model, the predicted relationships amongst these phenomena are believed to be similar cross-culturally (see Berry, 1992; 1998). However, as pointed out above this process may be more variable than theorized by Berry. Unfortunately, the empirical evidence is sorely lacking to either refute or support these relationships across the groups of interest. Because of the theoretical model, it is hypothesized that bicultural competence is related to adaptive processes and academic resilience via the mediating variables of stress and coping processes across contexts (i.e., social support coping in the familial context and direct action coping in the academic context).

The model also explores the possibility that bicultural competence has a direct rather than an indirect effect on adaptive processes (e.g., self-esteem) and academic resilience. Because of the theoretical model, it is hypothesized that bicultural competence is related to greater adaptive processes and academic resilience, regardless of stress and coping processes.

The alternative study and exploratory models explore the possibility that these expected relationships might not be evident. Models utilizing different variables (e.g., perceived parental warmth) and/or different configurations of the variables of interest may need to be generated. These models (i.e., alternative and exploratory) may provide a better explanation of the study findings than the original study model. The models are described further in Chapter 7.

In sum, this chapter presented an indirect/direct effects model of the predicted relationships amongst bicultural competence, stress and coping processes across contexts, adaptive processes (i.e., the exploratory variables of self-esteem and depressed mood), and academic resilience for both Latina/o and Southeast Asian adolescents. Alternative study models and exploratory models also were investigated herein to account for the study findings and to determine the best fitting model. The expected patterns for the inter- and intra-group comparisons, as well as the rationale for these hypotheses also were discussed.

CHAPTER 6

Between Group Comparisons

SAMPLE

Subjects were drawn from three socio-demographically distinct school sites in Northern and Central California. From the suburban high school site, 50 Latina/o (i.e., 47 Mexican, 2 Central American, 1 South American origins) and 48 Southeast Asian (i.e., 17 Laotian, 13 Vietnamese, 12 Cambodian, and 8 Thailand origins) 9th-grade, English speaking, male and female adolescents participated in the study. An additional 53 Latina/o (i.e., 50 Mexican and 3 Central American origins) and 41 Southeast Asian (i.e., 15 Laotian, 11 Vietnamese, 9 Cambodian, and 4 Thailand origins) 9th-grade, English speaking, male and female adolescents from an inner-city high school participated in the study (see Table 6-1 below for further family demographics). Also, 78 Latina/o (i.e., 76 Mexican, 1 Central American, and 1 South American origins) 9th-grade, English speaking, male and female adolescents from a rural middle school participated in only the factor analyses because their GPAs were unavailable for further analyses. No Southeast Asians participated in this study from this sample because there were only five eligible students at this site. In all, 270 questionnaires were administered to students.

Table 6-1 below reveals that the most common country of origin for the Southeast Asian was Laos (36%). For the Latinas/os, most subjects could trace their family origin to Mexico (89%) (also see Table 6-1). Most students were 14 years of age (77%) (M = 14.26 [SD = .55], range 13 – 17). The groups did not differ in gender composition. Of the Southeast Asian respondents, 62% were female; 38% were male. Of the Latina/o respondents, 60% were female and 40% were male. Chapter 7 contains further comparisons on demographics.

Table 6-1. Demographics: Family Origin Characteristics
<u>Family Origin</u>
Southeast Asian (<u>n</u> = 89)   Latina/o (<u>n</u> = 103)

Country	n	%	Country	n	%
Vietnam	24	26.9	Mexico	92	89.3
Cambodia	21	23.6	U.S.	5	4.9
Laos	32	35.9	Central America	3	2.9
Thailand	12	13.6	South America	3	2.9

PROCEDURE

All Students who were in the 9th-grade and who self-identified as Latina/o or Southeast Asian met the criteria for inclusion in the study. School site outreach and academic counselors designated by school administrators as liaisons or contact persons assisted in the identification of eligible students, and facilitated contacts between the researcher/research assistants and student participants. All eligible students listened to a short 15-minute presentation at their respective schools about the study and were given a packet of information consisting of an introductory statement and consent forms (see Appendix A) in English, Spanish, Mien, Hmong, and Vietnamese. Trained Latina/o and Southeast Asian undergraduate research assistants facilitated the presentations. Students were asked to write their names legibly on their consent forms for later identification for study participation. Further, students were encouraged to return the consent forms to their designated school liaisons as quickly as possible. Response rates across the school sites and ethnic groups ranged from 44% for the Latina/o and 44% for the Southeast Asian respondents at the suburban high school, 30% for the Latina/o and 49% for the Southeast Asian respondents at the inner-city high school, to 75% for the Latina/o respondents at the rural middle school.

The survey administration process commenced with the proper introductions, and explanations of the study and of the survey procedure, facilitated by the primary researcher and/or one to four highly trained Latina/o and/or Southeast Asian undergraduate research assistants. Significant efforts were made to develop rapport with the students, including the utilization of research assistants who were highly motivated and ethnically compatible, the provision of lunch, consisting of pizza and soft drinks, and the utilization of tactful self-disclosure. The surveys were administered at the school sites in unoccupied classrooms, offices, or auditoriums to groups of students ranging from 6 to 20 students after written self and parental permission had been secured. Students were asked to supply their names on separate pieces of paper for future follow-ups. A number corresponding to each participant's name was assigned to the questionnaires. Participants took approximately 30 to 45 minutes to complete the battery of questionnaires. At the completion of this procedure, each participant received $5.00 for their participation and was offered pizza and soda.

The suburban and inner-city high school data were collected during the first semester of students' 9th-grade academic year. The rural middle school site data were collected during the second semester of students' 9th-grade academic year. For this dissertation study, student participants were tracked for one academic year, from the beginning to the end of their 9th-grade year. At the end of the academic year, students' GPAs were recorded. A detailed log of this information was kept for each participant.

Measures

Appendix A consists of the English consent forms utilized on the participants and their parents. Appendix B consists of the questionnaire utilized in this study. A demographic questionnaire was administered to assess subjects' general background information. This questionnaire included questions on country(ies) of origin, sex, parental marital status, living situation, household income, and familial employment (see Tables 6-1, 7-1 to 7-5 and Appendix B). In all, 14 short one-sentence questions composed this part of the questionnaire.

Generation status was ascertained from question three of the demographic questionnaire (see Appendix B). This item sought to determine the country(ies) of birth of the participants and specified family members. This item was then recoded into 1 = immigrant, 2 = born in U.S., 3 = you and a parent born in the U.S., and 4 = you and a grandparent born in the U.S.

Familial SES was determined from question 12 of the demographic questionnaire (see Appendix B). This question was later divided into four separate items (father's job, mother's job, stepmother's job, and stepfather's job, if applicable) and recoded into 1 = unemployed, 2 = blue collar, and 3 = white collar.   Father's employment status was utilized to determine SES whenever appropriate (i.e., marriage intact). When subjects' fathers were not present and their mothers remained single, mother's employment status was utilized to determine SES. When subjects' mothers remarried, stepfather's employment status was utilized. The other items (e.g., question 13 on parental education) were not helpful in determining SES since only about 60% of the sample knew a parent's educational background (roughly 40% of the sample circled the unknown option).

To assess bicultural competence, the California Bicultural Competence Scale (CBCS) was developed (see Appendix B).   The CBCS was designed to assess bicultural competence in diverse ethnic groups in the United States. This measure underwent several revisions with two pilot studies before administration to the study sample; this process is discussed below.

The development of the scale involved three major steps. First, items were developed to reflect two cultural orientations: a White cultural domain and a non-specific ethnic cultural domain. Lafromboise, Coleman, and Gertons' (1993) criteria of assessing bicultural competence were utilized in constructing the items and dimensions of the CBCS. The following dimensions were explored in the pilot study phase: (1) knowledge of cultural beliefs and values of both the second culture and the culture of origin, (2) positive attitudes toward both majority and minority groups, (3) bicultural efficacy, (4) bilingual communication ability, (5) role repertoire, and (6) groundedness.

The items were refined with the second-phase of the pilot study, which consisted of several pilot studies conducted on both young and older adolescent samples. The items were initially shown to two focus groups – one in Northern California and the other in the Bay Area. Each group consisted of approximately six ethnically diverse adolescents between the ages of 13 and 15. Two professionals with clinical/research training and experience facilitated the groups. The youths offered helpful suggestions regarding the comprehensibility, construction, and relevance of the questions. For example, initially, we used the term "Anglo" in reference to Caucasians; however, the youths recommended the term "White" instead, which was considered in common use with youth. Furthermore, the term "ethnic" was problematic for some youth; therefore it was deemed necessary to define this construct before administration of the measure, especially with young adolescent samples.

The third-phase of the pilot study consisted of the application of the revised measure to a Northern California, college sample ($\underline{N}$ = 96). A total of 27 short one-sentence questions composed the measure at this stage of development. The sample was primarily Anglo (70%). Asian Americans and Latinas/os composed 17% and 13%, respectively, of the sample. Also, the sample was overwhelmingly female (94%) and between the ages of 19 and 23 (94%). Further, the sample tended to be well established as U.S. residents – 19% were first-generation, 26% were second-generation, 15% were third-generation, and 41% were fourth-generation. For this pilot study, we decided to keep the original term "Anglo" in reference to Caucasians because this term was thought to be more appropriate for a college student sample.

For this pilot study ($\underline{N}$ = 96), an exploratory principal-axis, factor analysis with varimax factor rotation was conducted. A varimax factor rotation was chosen for two reasons. For one, both varimax and oblimin factor rotations were attempted; upon inspection, the varimax rotation provided a stronger solution "structurally" (i.e., the factors were more distinct). Second, this rotation made more theoretical sense, since the theory on bicultural competence appears to suggest orthogonality, in other words, that there are at least two separate dimensions within this construct (i.e., an Anglo cultural orientation and an ethnic cultural orientation) (see LaFromboise et al., 1993).

The number of factors chosen was based on the scree-test, which indicated a three-dimensional factor structure for the college student, pilot study sample. Only items that had high item loadings (i.e., greater than .45) and greater loading onto one factor were utilized in this factor solution. Double-loaders also were not utilized in the factor solution. Because of this criterion, the following items were not included in the pilot study factor solution: (1) count on friends of own ethnic group to be there for help, (2) accept people of own ethnic group as close personal friends, (3) fluency in English, (4) speak English to friends, (5) knowledge of beliefs and values of the American culture, (6) good student, (7) responsibility for household chores, (8) responsibility for children, (9) participate in extracurricular activities, and (10) English/ethnic language translator. A total of 17 items were utilized in this factor solution.

Since none of the role repertoire items (e.g., participation in extracurricular activities) loaded significantly onto any of the factors, these five items were dropped from the pool of questionnaire items, bringing the total number of items down from 27 to 22. However, items 1-5 above were kept in the item pool because it was surmised that an ethnically diverse sample might respond differently to these items.

The three factors consisted of an Anglo identity and cultural orientation subscale, an ethnic identity and cultural orientation subscale, and an ethnic language subscale, accounting for 46% of the total variance. The first factor was the largest and accounted for 24% of the variance and consists of eight items. Factors two (6 items) and three (3 items) accounted for 13 percent and 9 percent of the variance, respectively. Table 6-2 below presents the factor loadings for the subscales for this pilot study. Recall that five items did not load significantly onto the factors but were kept in the questionnaire, and an additional five items were dropped from both the factor solution and the questionnaire.

Table 6-2. CBCS Pilot Study ($\underline{N}$ = 96) Factor Descriptions: Items in Decreasing Size of Factor Loadings (17 items)

Item No.	Factor Number: Description	Factor Loadings
Factor 1: Anglo Identity and Cultural Orientation		
23. Rely on Anglos for help		.93
12. Count on Anglo friends for help		.90
6. Positive feelings about Anglos		.84
5. Accept Anglos as friends		.75
16. Like to identify as American		.74
25. Appreciate Anglo values		.71
3. Proud to identify as American		.69
24. Speak English with family		.67
Factor 2: Ethnic Identity and Cultural Orientation		
27. Knowledge of ethnic group values		.75
11. Identify by own ethnicity		.68
13. Proud to identify by own ethnicity		.68
10. Appreciate values of ethnic group		.63
7. Rely on ethnic group for help		.62
8. Positive feelings about ethnic group		.61

Factor 3: Ethnic Language

22. Speak to family in own ethnic language	.86
15. Fluent in own ethnic language	.79
1. Speak to friends in ethnic language	.65

Items for each factor from the factor solution were subsequently grouped into subscales and tested for reliability. Table 6-3 below presents the Cronbach alpha reliability coefficients for each of the three subscales obtained on the pilot college student sample. The coefficients ranged from .81 to .92.

Table 6-3. Pilot Study ($\underline{N}$ = 96) Reliability Coefficients
for the CBCS Subscales

Subscale	Number of Items	Standardized Alpha Coefficient
Anglo Identity & Cultural Orientation	8	.92
Ethnic Identity & Cultural Orientation	6	.81
Ethnic Language	3	.85

Based on this pilot study, the CBCS appears to be multidimensional, consisting of at least three broad dimensions, but not the six dimensions theorized by LaFromboise et al. (1993), thus, providing partial support for the multidimensionality of this construct. However, since this factorial analysis was conducted on a college sample that was predominantly Anglo and not on a Latina/o or Southeast Asian high school student sample, further factor analyses of the CBCS were conducted with the sample of study. Studies find that factor solutions vary as a function of age, socioeconomic status, gender, and ethnicity, for example (see Dick, Beals, Keane, & Mason, 1994). Therefore, in addition to a combined ethnic factor analysis (i.e., Latina/o and Southeast Asian), separate ethnic specific factor analyses also were conducted. The sample was not large enough to conduct separate factor analyses for the different socioeconomic status levels and gender groups across the ethnic subsamples. Since most participants were 14 years of age (77%), age was not considered a factor for solution variability.

The fourth step consisted of the application of this revised scale to Latina/o and Southeast Asian 9th-grade adolescents (N = 270) from three socio-demographically distinct school sites in California, to psychometrically construct the bicultural competence scale and to establish its structural validity further. In all, 22 short one-sentence questions composed the final version of this questionnaire. Recall that LaFromboise et al.'s (1993) sixth criterion "role repertoire" of assessment of bicultural competence was not utilized in this phase of the study because this construct (i.e., 5 items) did not factor well on the pilot study discussed above.

A principal-axis, oblique rotation factor analysis was conducted, which accounted for 59% of the total variance. Both varimax and oblique factor rotations also were attempted; in this instance, an oblique factor rotation was deemed more appropriate because this solution made more sense structurally (i.e., the factors were more distinct). Also, this sample was thought to be more biculturally competent than the pilot study sample, which was primarily Anglo. According to LaFromboise et al. (1993), biculturally competent individuals are believed to embrace and integrate both cultural systems; hence, this rotation made more intuitive sense.

The number of factors chosen was based on the scree-test. For the combined ethnic factor analysis (Latina/o and Southeast Asian), the scree-test indicated a four- rather than a three-dimensional factor structure. All 22 items loaded significantly onto the four factors. The four factors consisted of an Anglo identity and cultural orientation subscale, an ethnic language subscale, an ethnic identity and cultural orientation subscale, and an English language subscale (see Table 6-4 below for the items that composed each factor). The first factor was the largest and accounted for 28% of the variance and consisted of eight items. Factors two (3 items), three (8 items), and four (3 items) accounted for 15%, 11%, and 5% of the variance, respectively.

Table 6-4. CBCS Entire Sample (N = 270) Factor Descriptions: Items
Listed in Decreasing Size of Factor Loadings (22 items)

Item No.	Factor Number: Description	Factor Loadings
Factor 1: Anglo Identity and Cultural Orientation		
5.	Positive feelings about White people	.77
21.	Appreciate beliefs or values held by White people	.73
19.	Rely on White people in general for help when needed	.72
11.	Count on White friends to be there when needed	.72
13.	Knowledge of the beliefs and values of the American culture	.68
4.	Accept White people as close personal friends	.68
15.	Like to identify as American	.52
2.	Proud to identify as American	.48
Factor 2: Ethnic Language		
18.	Speak to family in own ethnic language	.88
14.	Fluent in own ethnic language	.84
1.	Speak to friends in a language other than English	.65
Factor 3: Ethnic Identity and Cultural Orientation		
17.	Count on friends of own ethnic group when needed	-.75
8.	Accept people of own ethnic group as close personal friends	-.72
6.	Rely on own ethnic group for help when needed	-.70
7.	Positive feelings about people of own ethnic group	-.67
12.	Proud to identify by own ethnicity	-.66
10.	Like to identify by own ethnicity	-.59
9.	Appreciate beliefs or values held by those of own ethnic group	-.56
22.	Knowledge of beliefs and values of own ethnic group	-.50
Factor 4: Anglo Language		
3.	Speak English to friends	.73
16.	Fluent in English	.69
20.	Speak English with family	.51

Items for each factor from the factor analysis also were grouped
into subscales and tested for reliability. Cronbach alpha reliability

coefficients were .86 for the Anglo identity and cultural orientation subscale, .83 for the ethnic language subscale, .86 for the ethnic identity and cultural orientation subscale, and .77 for the Anglo language subscale (see Table 6-5 below).

Table 6-5. Entire Sample ($\underline{N}$ = 270) Reliability Coefficients
for the CBCS Subscales

Subscale	Number of items	Standardized Alpha Coefficient
Anglo Identity & Cultural Orientation	8	.86
Ethnic Language	3	.83
Ethnic Identity & Cultural Orientation	8	.85
Anglo Language	3	.77

For the Latina/o ($\underline{n}$ = 181) principal-axis factor analysis, an oblique factor rotation was deemed appropriate also for the same reasons. The number of factors chosen was based on the scree-test, which indicated a four-factor solution. All 22 items also loaded significantly onto the four factors. The four factors were similar to the combined ethnic factor solution, consisting of an Anglo identity and cultural orientation subscale, an ethnic language subscale, an ethnic identity and cultural orientation subscale, and an Anglo language subscale (see Table 6-6 for the items that composed each factor). The four factors accounted for 59% of the total variance. The first factor was the largest and accounted for 28% of the total variance and consisted of eight items. Factors two (3 items), three (8 items), and four (3 items) accounted for 15%, 11%, and 5% of the total variance, respectively.

Table 6-6. CBCS Latina/o (n = 181) Factor Descriptions: Items Listed in Decreasing Size of Factor Loadings (22 items)

Item No.	Factor Number: Description	Factor Loadings
Factor 1: Anglo Identity and Cultural Orientation		
5.	Positive feelings about White people	.77
21.	Appreciate beliefs or values held by White people	.73
19.	Rely on White people in general for help when needed	.72
11.	Count on White friends to be there when needed	.72
13.	Knowledge of the beliefs and values of the American culture	.68
4.	Accept White people as close personal friends	.68
15.	Like to identify as American	.52
2.	Proud to identify as American	.48
Factor 2: Ethnic Language		
18.	Speak to family in own ethnic language	.88
14.	Fluent in own ethnic language	.84
1.	Speak to friends in a language other than English	.65
Factor 3: Ethnic Identity and Cultural Orientation		
17.	Count on friends of own ethnic group to be there when needed	-.75
8.	Accept people of own ethnic group as close personal friends	-.72
6.	Rely on own ethnic group for help when needed	.70
7.	Positive feelings about people of own ethnic group	-.67
12.	Proud to identify by own ethnicity	-.66
10.	Like to identify by own ethnicity	-.59
9.	Appreciate beliefs or values held by those of own ethnic group	-.56
22.	Knowledge of beliefs and values of own ethnic group	-.50
Factor 4: Anglo Language		
3.	Speak English to friends	.73
16.	Fluent in English	.69
20.	Speak English with family	.51

Items for each factor from the Latina/o ethnic specific factor analysis also were grouped into subscales and tested for reliability. Cronbach alphas were .88 for the Anglo identity and cultural orientation subscale, .88 for the ethnic language subscale, .83 for the ethnic identity and cultural orientation subscale, and .79 for the Anglo language subscale (see Table 6-7 below).

Table 6-7. Reliability Coefficients for the Latina/o ($\underline{n}$ = 181) CBCS Subscales

Subscale	Number of items	Standardized Alpha Coefficient
Anglo Identity & Cultural Orientation Subscale	8	.88
Ethnic Language Subscale	3	.88
Ethnic Identity & Cultural Orientation Subscale	8	.83
Anglo Language Subscale	3	.79

For the Southeast Asian ($\underline{n}$ = 89) principal-axis factor analysis, an oblique factor rotation also seemed structurally appropriate. The number of factors chosen was based on the scree-test, which clearly indicated at least two separate, rather large factors. Only items that had high item loadings (i.e., greater than .45) and greater loading onto one factor were utilized in this solution. Double-loaders also were not utilized in this factor solution. Based on this criterion, only one item was eliminated from this analysis but not from the item pool; this was item 1, "Speak to friends in a language other than English".

Three- and four-factor solutions were attempted; however, the additional factors were weak – each lacked coherence or consisted of relatively few items. This result could be an artifact of the relatively smaller size of this subsample as compared to the Latina/o subsample (89 vs. 181, respectively). In this instance, the two-factor solution was superior, consisting of a general Anglo cultural orientation subscale and a general ethnic cultural orientation subscale (see Table 6-8 below for the items that composed each factor). Each subscale was composed of behavioral, value/attitudinal, and language items. The two factors accounted for 44% of the total variance. The first factor was the largest, accounting for 32% of the total variance (11 items), while the second factor accounted for 12% of the total variance (10 items).

Table 6-8. CBCS Southeast Asian ($\underline{n}$ = 89) Factor Descriptions: Items Listed in Decreasing Size of Factor Loadings (21 items)

Item No.	Factor Number: Description	Factor Loadings
Factor 1: General Anglo Cultural Orientation		
5.	Positive feelings about White people	.69
20.	Speak English with family	.67
13.	Knowledge of the beliefs and values of the American culture	.64
4.	Accept White people as close personal friends	.62
21.	Appreciate beliefs or values held by White people	.62
16.	Fluent in English	.60
15.	Like to identify as American	.57
19.	Rely on White people in general for help when needed	.56
11.	Count on White friends to be there when needed	.55
3.	Speak English to friends	.51
2.	Proud to identify as American	.51
Factor 2: General Ethnic Cultural Orientation		
17.	Count on friends of own ethnic group to be there when needed	.75
6.	Rely on own ethnic group for help when needed	.72
7.	Positive feelings about people of own ethnic group	.68
12.	Proud to identify by own ethnicity	.66
8.	Accept people of own ethnic group as close personal friends	.59
9.	Appreciate beliefs or values held by those of own ethnic group	.56
18.	Speak to family in own ethnic language	.55
14.	Fluent in own ethnic language	.53
10.	Like to identify by own ethnicity	.51
22.	Knowledge of beliefs and values of own ethnic group	.48

Items for each factor from the Southeast Asian ethnic specific factor analysis also were grouped into subscales and tested for reliability. Cronbach alpha reliability coefficients were .86 for the general Anglo cultural orientation subscale and .86 for the general ethnic cultural orientation subscale (see Table 6-9 below).

Table 6-9. Reliability Coefficients for the Southeast Asian ($n = 89$) CBCS Subscales

Subscale	Number of items	Standardized Alpha Coefficient
General Anglo Cultural Orientation	11	.86
General Ethnic Cultural Orientation	10	.86

Although the factor solutions varied across the two ethnic subsamples, for this study the combined Latina/o and Southeast Asian factor solution (N = 270) was utilized for the following reasons. First, the Southeast Asian subsample lacked sufficient power (n = 89) necessary to adequately determine the CBCS' factor structure with this ethnic group. Because of this limitation, it is not clear whether a different facto solution (i.e., 4-factor solution) may have been evident had the sample greater power. Therefore, for this reason and to conserve statistical power, the decision to utilize a combined ethnic factor solution was arrived at. Second, the study attempted to test the relevance of a cross-cultural model (see Figure 5-1 in Chapter 5). This model is theorized to apply cross-culturally.

To create a bicultural competence scale (i.e., high on both an Anglo and an ethnic cultural orientation), the following procedure was undertaken. First, utilizing the combined ethnic (i.e., Latina/o and Southeast Asian) factor structure solution, two matrices were created – one for language and another for identity/cultural orientation. Each matrix was then divided into an ethnic language or ethnic identity/cultural orientation on the horizontal axis and an English or Anglo identity/cultural orientation on the vertical axis. Each index was subsequently divided into tertiles (low, medium, and high). Each case was then assigned a score based upon its position on or off diagonals.

For example, a low-level ethnic language score and a low-level English language score was assigned a "1", a mid-level ethnic language score and mid-level English language score was assigned a "3", a mid-level English language score and a high-level ethnic language score was assigned a "5", and a high-level ethnic language and a high-level English language score was assigned a "6". In this way, two "bicultural" composite dimensions were created, consisting of a language dimension and an identity/values dimension (see Tables 6-10 and 6-11 below).

Table 6-10. CBCS – Language Dimension – Scoring Index
Ethnic Language

	Low Scores: (3-8)	Mid (9-10)	High (11-15)
Low (3-11)	1	2	4
English Mid Language (12-13)	2	3	5
High (14-15)	4	5	6

Table 6-11. CBCS – Identity/Values Dimension – Scoring Index

<u>Ethnic Identity/Values</u>

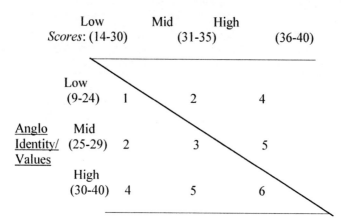

	Low Scores: (14-30)	Mid (31-35)	High (36-40)
Low (9-24)	1	2	4
Anglo Identity/ Values Mid (25-29)	2	3	5
High (30-40)	4	5	6

Table 6-12 reveals that the mean for the bicultural competence language dimension was 21.89 with a standard deviation of 9.76. The means were 12.28 for the Anglo language factor and 9.61 for the ethnic language factor with standard deviations of 2.37 for the Anglo language factor and 3.29 for the ethnic language factor (also see Table 6-12). Table 6-12 also reveals that the reliability coefficient for the English language factor was .77 and .83 for the ethnic language factor.

Table 6-12. Sample (Combined Ethnic Groups) Means,
Standard Deviations, and Alphas for Items/Subscales/Scales

<u>Index</u>	<u>n</u>	<u>Mean</u>	<u>Standard Deviation</u>	<u>Alpha</u>
CBCS (factors):				
Anglo Language	92	12.28	2.37	.77
Ethnic Language	192	9.61	3.29	.83
Anglo Identity & Values	192	27.44	6.23	.86
Ethnic Identity & Values	192 3	2.62	5.31	.81

CBCS-Language Dimension	192	21.89	9.76	N/A
CBCS-Identity & Values Dimension	192	60.06	9.40	N/A
Measure of Daily Coping: Familial Social Support	186	1.46	1.19	N/A
Academic Direct Action	186	1.85	1.09	N/A
CES D	192	8.39	4.10	.74
Rosenberg's Self Esteem Scale	192	22.79	4.08	.74
Academic Goals	192	57.75	8.15	.88
Perceived Parental Warmth	192	27.18	6.19	.85
CSES-School Support	192	32.71	5.80	.83
CSES-Perceived School Discrimination	192	11.80	4.29	.74

Table 6-12 above also reveals that the mean for the bicultural competence identity/values dimension was 60.06 with a standard deviation of 9.40. The means were 27.44 for the Anglo identity/values factor and 32.62 for the ethnic identity/values factor with standard deviations of 6.23 for the Anglo identity/values factor and 5.31 for the ethnic identity/values factor. Table 6-12 also reveals that the reliability coefficient for the Anglo identity/values factor was .86 and .81 for the ethnic identity/values factor.

Although the factor solutions varied across the two ethnic subsamples, the combined Latina/o and Southeast Asian factor solution was utilized to determine validity for the aforementioned reasons. Criterion validity was determined by correlating the CBCS factors and subscales with respondents' generational status. Respondents' generational status has been used extensively to determine criterion validity of acculturation scales (see Cuellar, Harris, & Jasso, 1980;

Deyo, Diehl, Hazuda, & Stern, 1985; Marin, Sabogal, Van Oss Marin, Otero-Sabogal, Perez-Stable, 1987; Olmedo & Padilla, 1978; Padilla, 1980; Szapocznik, Scopetta, Kurtines, & Aranalde, 1978; Triadis, Kashima, Hui, Lisansk, & Marin, 1982). Olmedo (1979) posits that "individual acculturation should be a direct function of the amount of exposure to the host culture for . . . the particular subgroup to which the individual belongs (e.g., generational distance from time of immigration)" (p. 1068) (cited in Marin et al., 1987).

Not surprisingly, the ethnic language factor was inversely correlated with generational status (r = -.54), whereas the English language factor was positively correlated (r = .41). However, of the two identity and cultural orientation factors, only the Anglo identity and cultural orientation factor correlated significantly with generational status (r = .21). Interestingly, the ethnic identity and cultural orientation factor was unrelated to generational status (r = .06). Of the bicultural competence dimensions, only the CBCS identity and cultural orientation dimension correlated with generational status (r = .22). The CBCS language dimension was unrelated to generational status.

It is possible that the non-significant correlations reflect a non-linear relationship between language use and generational status. It is reasonable to expect that the second generation might be more bicultural than either the first or the third generations. Thus, one-way ANOVAs were conducted to examine mean differences in bicultural competence factors and dimensions by generational status, testing for polynomial effects. The ethnic language factor did show a significant weighted quadratic term, $F(1, 188) = 7.18$, $p < .01$, with the first and second generations being much higher in ethnic language competence than the 3rd and 4th. As expected, the mean for the CBCS language dimension was highest for the second generation, but the weighted quadratic term did not achieve significance, $F(1, 188) = 1.77$, ns.

To assess stress and coping processes across contexts, the following procedure was undertaken. Subjects were asked to report on two recent stressful events, one occurring at home in the familial context and another occurring at school in the academic context. Also, subjects were asked to provide brief descriptions of these stressors on a questionnaire and to provide the approximate dates of the stressful events. These items had been developed and utilized previously by Aldwin, Sutton, and Lachman (1996).

Regarding the coding of students' open-ended descriptions of stressors across contexts, a content analysis was conducted by this researcher and four undergraduate research assistants on a quarter of the completed questionnaire, resulting in the following categories: (1) minor problem (e.g., hassle and argument), (2) work/school related problem (e.g., grades and work overload), (3) relational problem (e.g., triangulation and individuation), (4) loss (e.g., death of relative/friend, parental divorce, and migration experience), and (5) major problem (e.g., violence or abuse).

Inter-rater reliability of .80 was achieved amongst these researchers, utilizing this scoring system on ten randomly chosen questionnaires. The questionnaires were then divided amongst four research assistants who were given the task of coding the stressors across contexts into the aforementioned categories. These researchers then traded groups of questionnaires to code a second time around. Inconsistencies in coding the stressors across contexts were resolved in weekly lab meetings. A fifth researcher conducted random quality checks of researchers' coding responses.

Subjects also were asked on the questionnaire to rate the stressfulness of the events (from 1 = little or no stress to 7 = most stress), again utilizing an item from Aldwin et al. (1996). Participants were then asked to appraise the stressful events (e.g., as threat, harm, loss, challenge, or annoyance), utilizing an item also from Aldwin et al. Further, subjects were asked on the questionnaire to identify the strategies used to cope with the events, utilizing Stone and Neale's eight-item Measure of Daily Coping (1984) (see below for further details on this measure). Finally, participants were asked to rate how well they coped with the situations (from 1 = not well at all to 5 = very well), utilizing another item from Aldwin et al.

To assess consistency of coping across contexts, a repeated measures design utilizing Aldwin et al.'s (1996) items and the Measure of Daily Coping in the family versus academic context, was utilized. In all, 10 questions across two contexts (i.e., familial and academic) composed the stress and coping questionnaire utilized in this study.

Regarding Stone and Neale's (1984) eight-item Measure of Daily Coping, this scale was previously utilized by Aldwin and Greenberger (1987) to assess psychosocial predictors of depression among ethnic Korean and Caucasian students with favorable results. The scale also was utilized by Compas, Forsythe, and Wagner (1988) in a study of coping consistency in adolescents.

Stone and Neale (1984) factor analyzed their inventory and found eight dimensions or different types of coping, which were utilized in this study, these are: (1) Distraction: "turned my attention away from the problem by thinking about other things or getting involved in some activity"; (2) Situation redefinition: "tried to see the problem in a different light that made it seem more bearable"; (3) Direct action: "thought about solutions to the problem and did something to solve it"; (4) Catharsis: "expressed feelings in response to the problem to reduce tension, anxiety, or frustration"; (5) Acceptance: "accepted that the problem had occurred, but that nothing could be done"; (6) Seeking social support: "sought or found emotional social support from loved ones, friends, or professionals"; (7) Relaxation: "did something with the specific purpose of relaxing"; and (8) Religion: "sought or found spiritual or religious comfort".

In all, eight strategies were offered to participants as coping options. The eight-item checklist was modified by the addition of a frequency rating scale, where "0" indicated that the respondent had not used that particular strategy at all to "3" that the respondent had used that strategy a lot.

A total of 186 subjects completed this measure and responded to the items. Interestingly, six subjects had no stressful and subsequently no coping processes to report on across contexts. Table 6-12 reveals that the mean for familial social support coping was 1.46 with a standard deviation of 1.19. The mean for academic direct action coping was 1.85 with a standard deviation of 1.09 (also see Table 6-12). Reliability coefficients were not generated for the Measure of Daily Coping since this measure utilized only one item to assess each coping strategy.

Self-esteem was an exploratory outcome variable in the original study model and a mediating variable in the alternative and exploratory models (see Chapter 5). To assess self-esteem, Rosenberg's Self-Esteem Scale (1965) was utilized. The following items, rated on a scale from 1 = strongly disagree to 4 = strongly agree, were utilized in this study: (1) "On the whole, I am satisfied with myself"; (2) "I am able to do things as well as most other people"; (3) "I feel that I have a number of good qualities"; (4) "I wish I could have more respect for myself (reverse coded)"; (5) "I take a positive attitude toward myself"; (6) "At times, I think I am no good at all (reverse coded)"; (7) "All in all, I am inclined to feel that I'm a failure (reverse coded)"; and (8) "I feel that I'm a person of worth, at least on an equal plane with others".

Table 6-12 above presents the means, standard deviation, and alpha for this instrument. The mean was 22.79 with a standard deviation of 4.08. Internal reliability for this scale was .74 for this study.

Depressed mood was an exploratory outcome variable in the original study model and a mediating variable in the alternative and exploratory models (see Chapter 5). To assess depressed mood, the Center for Epidemiological Studies Depression Scale (CES D) (Radloff, 1971) was utilized in the study. The following items, rated on a scale from 0 = hardly ever or never to 2 = much or most of the time, were utilized: (1) "" did not feel like eating: my appetite was poor"" (2) "I felt depressed"; (3) "I felt everything I did was an effort"; (4) "My sleep was restless"; (5) "I was happy (reverse coded)"; (6) "I felt lonely"; (7) "People were unfriendly"; (8) "I enjoyed life (reverse coded)"; (9) "I felt sad"; (10) "I felt that people disliked me"; and (11) "I could not 'get going'".

Table 6-12 above presents the mean, standard deviation, and alpha for this scale as well. The mean was 8.39 with a standard deviation of 4.10. Internal reliability for the scale was .74 for the study.

"Academic goals" was an exploratory variable utilized as a mediating variable in the exploratory model along with self-esteem and depressed mood. To assess academic goals, Fuligni's (1997) items on self (adolescents') and perceived parental value of academic success were utilized. In all, 14 items, rated on a scale from 1 = not at all to 5 = a great deal, were utilized in this study. The perceived parental value of academic success items consisted of the following questions, phrased by "How important is it to your parent(s) that you": do well in school/graduate from high school/get good grades/go to college after high school/get an 'A' on almost every test/be one of the best students in your class/go to the best college after high school". The adolescents' value of academic success items consisted of the following questions, phrased by "How important is it to you to": graduate from high school/do well in school/get good grades/get an 'A' on almost every test/be one of the best students in your class/go to the best college after high school/go to college after high school?

Since the perceived parental and adolescents' value of academic success dimensions wee highly correlated (r = .64, p < .01) and a factor analysis failed to find two distinct factors (i.e., a perceived parental academic goals factor and a self or adolescents' academic goals factor), the two dimensions were combined. Table 6-12 presents the mean, standard deviation, and alpha for this measure. The mean for this scale was 57.75, with a standard deviation of 8.15. Internal reliability for the scale was .88 for the study.

"Perceptions of parental warmth" was an environmental variable utilized in this study in an exploratory model (see Chapter 5). To assess perceived parental warmth, seven items were developed to reflect perceptions of maternal, paternal, and familial warmth. The following items, rated on a scale from 1 = not at all to 5 = a great deal, were utilized: (1) "How close are you to your mother?"; (2) "How close are you to your father?"; (3) "How caring is your mother to you?"; (4) "How caring is your father to you?"; (5) "How satisfied are you with your relationship with your mother?"; (6) "How satisfied are you with your relationship with your father?"; and (7) "How much do you feel loved and wanted by your closest family members?".

Perceived maternal warmth was significantly correlated with perceived paternal warmth ($r = .54$, $p < .01$); hence the items were combined into one global parental scale. Table 6-12 reveals that the mean for this scale was 27.18 with a standard deviation of 6.19. This table also reveals that the internal reliability for the scale was .85 for the study.

"Perceived school discrimination" was the last environmental variable utilized in this study in an exploratory model (see Chapter 5). The California School Environment Scale (CSES) was developed and utilized to assess perceptions of school discrimination. The scale consists of 21 short, one-sentence questions, rated on a scale from 1 = not at all to 5 = a great deal, which was designed to assess not only perceptions of school discrimination but also perceived school support. However, only the perceptions of school discrimination dimension was utilized in the study. Attempts were made to incorporate this variable into the environmental exploratory model; however, this model was not significant (i.e., fit tests indicated a poor fit of this model to the data); hence this variable was dropped from the analysis. The items were based on the Latino Commission and Fordham University Survey on the Latino Dropout Crisis (Rodriquez, 1992). Minor surface changes were made to the items drawn from this pool to condense them and improve clarity (e.g., removing negative such as "not"), and a likert rating scale was added.

A pilot study was conducted on an earlier version of the CSES, which consisted of 27 items. This pilot study was composed of 96 primarily Anglo (70%) (Asian Americans: 17% and Latinas/os: 13%), female (94%), college students between the ages of 19 and 23 (94%). A principal-axis factor analysis with varimax rotation was conducted on this pilot study sample. The scree-test indicated a three-factor solution for this pilot study, which accounted for 40 percent of the total variance. The three factors consisted of a perceived school discrimination factor (15 percent of the variance), a perceived school support factor (14 percent of the variance), and a perceived gender discrimination factor (11 percent of the variance). This last factor, "perceived gender discrimination," was not utilized in the current study because this questionnaire had to be condensed for a younger sample. Further, for the current study, one item was added, which was "in general, how much do you respect your teachers?"

Regarding the current study, a factor analysis was conducted on the CSES ($\underline{N}$ =270) to determine its structure with a more ethnically diverse sample (i.e., Latina/o and Southeast Asian). A principal-axis factor analysis with varimax factor rotation was deemed appropriate because school discrimination and school support were believed to be orthogonal or separate dimensions. The number of factors chosen was based on the scree-test, which indicated a two-factor solution. Only items that had high item loadings (greater than .45) and greater loading onto one factor were utilized in the factor solution. Double-loaders also were excluded from the factor solution.

Because of this criterion, the following items were not included in this factor solution: (1) like this school, (2) ethnic culture respected at school, (3) clarity on what to do to graduate, (4) sensitivity of teachers to cultural differences at school, (5) see an academic counselor at school, (6) ethnic culture celebrated at school, and (7) seen a student hit or attack another student at school. In sum, seven items were excluded from only the factor solution, leaving a total of 17 items in this factor solution.

The two factors consisted of a perceived school support factor and a perceived school discrimination factor (see Table 6-13 below for the items that composed each factor). The two factors accounted for 30% of the total variance. The first factor, consisting of nine items, was the largest and accounted for 19% of the total variance. Factor two, consisting of five items, accounted for 11% of the total variance.

Table 6-13. CSES Entire Sample (N = 270) Factor Description
Items Listed in Decreasing Size of Factor Loadings (14 items)

Item No.	Factor Number: Description	Factor Loadings
Factor 1: Perceived School Support		
17.	Teachers encourage you to continue your education	.72
4.	Teachers care about students at your school	.72
3.	Teachers treat students with respect at your school	.68
19.	Teachers expect you to do your best at school	.65
21.	You respect your teachers	.63
13.	Teachers give you one-on-one help with your work	.55
2.	School helping you get ready for what you want to do after you graduate	.55
18.	How safe is your school for your physical well-being	.53
16.	Different ethnic groups at your school get along with one another	.46
Factor 2: Perceived School Discrimination		
14.	Students at your school not treated fairly by teachers because of their ethnicity	.74
20.	Afraid that someone will hit or hurt you because of your ethnicity	.68
12.	Feel uncomfortable at your school because of your ethnicity	.66
11.	Students at your school not treated fairly by other Students because of their ethnicity	.56
6.	Afraid that someone will hurt or bother you at your school	.45

Items for each factor from the CSES were grouped into the two subscales and tested for reliability. Cronbach alpha reliability coefficients were .83 for the perceived school support subscale and .74 for the perceived school discrimination subscale (see Table 6-14 below).

Table 6-14. Entire Sample ($\underline{N}$ = 270) Reliability Coefficients
for the CSES Subscales

Subscale	Number of items	Standardized Alpha Coefficient
Perceived School Support	9	.83
Perceived School Discrimination	5	.74

Table 6-12 above presents the means, standard deviations, and alphas for the perceived school discrimination subscale and for the perceived school support subscale. The mean for the perceived school discrimination subscale was 11.80 with a standard deviation of 4.29. The mean for the perceived school support subscale was 32.71 with a standard deviation of 5.80. Internal reliability is given above and in Table 6-14.

Regarding the academic outcome variable, to assess academic resilience, students' official GPAs were obtained from school records at the end of the academic year.

Analyses

Means and standard deviations for each item/subscale/scale (e.g., self-esteem, bicultural competence – language dimension, and coping efficacy) were computed separately for each ethnic subgroup and for the combined ethnic groups (i.e., Latina/o and Southeast Asian). Mean substitution was utilized to deal with missing data. As previously mentioned, several participants had no stressful situations to report on the stress and coping across contexts items and measure. Mean substitution was not utilized in these cases. These subjects were excluded in all analyses relevant to the variables of stress and coping processes across contexts.

Group differences on the items/subscales/scales were dealt with the $\underline{X}^2$, $\underline{t}$-, and $\underline{F}$-tests. For some of the between-groups comparisons, a multivariate analysis (MANCOVA) was conducted with ethnicity (two levels for Latinas/os and Southeast Asians) as the dependent variable (1 DV) and CBCS-language and –identity/values dimensions as the independent variables (2 IVs), controlling for generational status (self) and familial SES.

To determine the internal structure of the CBCS and the CSES, principal-axis factor analyses were conducted on the combined sample and/or groups (i.e., Latina/o and Southeast Asian) as mentioned earlier. Pearson product-moment correlations for all possible combinations of the bicultural competence indices, stress and coping processes across contexts items and indices, self-esteem scale, depressed mood scale, self and perceived parental academic goals dimensions, perceived parental warmth index, perceived school discrimination subscale, and GPA were conducted.

Structural equation analyses were conducted on the data to test the relevance of the original study model, two alternative study models, and an exploratory model. James, Mulaik, and Brett (1982) explain that this type of analysis is a form of regression analysis that estimates the direct and indirect causal relationships among variables. Since the models attempted to utilize both indirect and direct effects paths, this type of analysis was deemed appropriate. For the original study model, the indirect effects path explore the possibility that bicultural competence may have an indirect effect on academic resilience (i.e., GPA) via the mediating variables of stress and coping processes across contexts. On the other hand, the direct effects path explored the possibility that bicultural competence may have a direct effect on academic resilience (i.e., GPA), regardless of these mediating variables. For sake of simplicity, this model was tested separately for each domain (i.e., familial and academic contexts). However, these models poorly fitted the data. Hence, alternative study models, which explored these same variables (i.e., bicultural competence, stress and coping processes across contexts, self-esteem, depressed mood, and academic resilience), but in different configurations, were generated separately for each context in Chapter 7. Nevertheless, a composite model of the original study model, which was tested, is presented in Chapter 7 for comparative purposes.

The relevance of a number of exploratory variables (i.e., self-esteem, depressed mood, self and perceived parental academic goals, perceived parental warmth, and perceived school discrimination) in the original study model, the alternative study models, and in an exploratory model also were explored herein. These variables were utilized as predictor, mediating, and outcome variables of and along with GPA in the models. The exploratory model was investigated herein to ascertain whether a different model represented the data better than the original study model and the alternative study models. To determine the goodness of fit of the path models, the following fit tests were utilized: $\underline{X}^2$ with probability level, Root Mean Square of Approximation (RMSEA), the Comparative Fit Index (CFI), and the Relative Fit Index (RFI).

CHAPTER 7
Results

In this chapter, comparisons between the Latina/o and Southeast Asian groups on demographics and on measures of bicultural competence, stress and coping processes across contexts, self-esteem, depressed mood, academic goals, perceived parental warmth, perceived school discrimination, and GPA will be discussed first. Next, within-group associations amongst these indices for the combined ethnic groups sample (N = 192) will be addressed, followed by a brief discussion of the rationale for combining the groups in these analyses. Finally, the results of the structural equation analyses examining indirect and direct effects models will be presented.

DEMOGRAPHIC GROUP COMPARISONS

Significant group differences were evident for place of birth. Table 7-1 below reveals that most of the Latinas/os were born in the U.S. (81%) compared to only 54% of the Southeast Asians. Only 19% of the Latina/o participants were born outside of the U.S., whereas 46% of the Southeast Asian students were born outside the U.S. It appears that the Latinas/os were more likely to be born in the U.S., in contrast to the Southeast Asians who were more evenly split in terms of place of birth, $\underline{X}^2$ (1, 192) = 15.64, $\underline{p}$ < .001.

Table 7-1. Demographics: Ethnic Characteristics

Group Characteristics	Southeast Asian (n = 89)		Latina/o (n = 103)		
	n	%	n	%	X^2
Place of Birth					
United States	48	53.9	83	80.6	
Outside U.S.	41	46.1	20	19.4	15.64***
Generation Level					
First (immigrant)	41	46.1	21	20.4	
Second	47	52.8	25	24.3	
Third	0	0	35	34.0	
Fourth	1	1	22	21.3	66.68***

***p < .001.

Not surprisingly, the respondents also differed in terms of generational status. Table 7-1 above also reveals that Southeast Asian respondents were more likely to be first and second generation, in contrast to the Latina/o participants who were more evenly split amongst first, second, third, and fourth generational status, X^2 (3, 192) = 66.68, p < .001. The Southeast Asians appear to be an immigrant sample, whereas the Latina/o respondents were more mixed in terms of generational status.

Despite the fact that the Southeast Asian group was more likely to be an immigrant sample, there were no significant group differences for enrollment in English as a Second Language (ESL) courses. Table 7-2 below reveals that only 26% of the Southeast Asian and 24% of the Latina/o respondents wee enrolled in ESL courses according to official academic records. Most were not enrolled in these courses (Southeast Asian: 74% and Latina/o: 76%).

Table 7-2. Demographics: Academic Characteristics

Group Characteristic	Southeast Asian ($\underline{n}$ = 89)		Latina/o ($\underline{n}$ = 103)		
	$\underline{n}$	%	$\underline{n}$	%	X^2
ESL					
Yes	23	25.8	25	24.3	
No	66	74.2	78	75.7	0.06
College Prep Classes					
Yes	79	88.8	100	97.1	
No	10	11.2	3	2.9	5.24*
Grade Advancement					
Passed	87	97.8	89	86.4	
Retained	2	2.2	14	13.6	8.05**

*$\underline{p}$ < .05. **$\underline{p}$ < .01.

Interestingly, although the groups did not differ on enrollment in ESL courses, the groups did differ in college preparatory course enrollment and in grade advancement according to official school records. Table 7-2 above also reveals that more Latinas/os (97%) were enrolled in college preparatory courses than Southeast Asians (89%). Latinas/os were more likely to be enrolled in college preparatory courses than the Southeast Asians, X^2 (1, 192) = 5.24, $\underline{p}$ < .05. Nevertheless, more Southeast Asians (98%) advanced in grade than Latinas/os (86%). Southeast Asian respondents, despite both an immigrant status and less likelihood of enrolling in college preparatory courses, were more likely to advance in grade than the Latina/o participants, X^2 (1, 192) = 8.05, $\underline{p}$ < .01.

Significant group differences also were found for socioeconomic status (SES). Tables 7-3, 7-4, and 7-5 below reveal that the Southeast Asian families were more likely to be impoverished. Parents of the Southeast Asian respondents wee more likely to be unemployed (mothers: 67%; fathers: 52%) than the parents of the Latina/o respondents (mothers: 23%; fathers: 4%), mothers: X^2 (3, 188) = 52.24, p < .001, fathers: X^2 (3, 190) = 57.55, p < .001. Also, Southeast Asian respondents' parents were more likely to not have an education (mothers: 28%; fathers: 21%) than Latinas/os subjects' parents (mothers: 1%; fathers: 3%), mothers: X^2 (4, 191) = 74.67, p < .001, fathers: X^2 (4, 191) = 34.37, p < .001. Further, Southeast Asian families were more likely to be on welfare than Latina/o families (67% vs. 5%, respectively), X^2 (1, 192) = 83.45, p < .001. Furthermore, Southeast Asian families were more likely to be larger in size than Latina/o families, X^2 (3, 192) = 28.30, p < .001.

Table 7-3. Demographics: Mother's SES Characteristics

Group Characteristic	Southeast Asian (n = 89)		Latina/o (n = 103)		
	n	$\%$	n	$\%$	X^2
Mother's Job					
White-collar	6	6.7	32	32.3	
Blue-collar	12	13.5	40	40.4	
Unemployed	60	67.4	23	23.2	
Unknown	11	12.4	4	4.1	52.24***
Mother's Education					
None	25	28.1	1	1.0	
$1^{st} - 8^{th}$ grade	2	2.2	11	10.8	
High school	19	21.3	43	42.2	
College	10	11.2	41	40.2	
Unknown	33	37.1	6	5.9	74.67***

***p < .001.

Table 7-4.
Demographics: Father's SES Characteristics

Group Characteristic	Southeast Asian ($\underline{n}$ = 89)		Latina/o ($\underline{n}$ = 103)		
	$\underline{n}$	$\underline{\%}$	$\underline{n}$	$\underline{\%}$	$\underline{X^2}$
Father's Job					
White-collar	10	11.2	26	25.7	
Blue-collar	19	21.3	51	50.5	
Unemployed	46	51.7	4	4.0	
Unknown	14	15.7	20	19.8	57.55***
Father's Education					
None	19	21.3	3	2.9	
$1^{st} - 8^{th}$ grade	0	0	9	8.8	
High school	18	20.2	44	43.1	
College	20	22.5	26	25.5	
Unknown	32	36.0	20	19.6	34.37***

***$\underline{p}$ < .001.

Table 7-5. Demographics: Household Characteristics

Characteristic	Southeast Asian (n = 89)		Latina/o (n = 103)		
	n	%	n	%	X^2
Household Income					
Welfare	60	67.4	5	4.9	
Earned income	29	32.6	98	95.1	83.45***
Household Size					
Small (under 4)	11	12.4	39	37.9	
Medium (4 - 5)	12	13.5	25	24.3	
Large (5 – 6)	18	20.2	16	15.5	
Extra-large (6+)	48	53.9	23	22.3	28.30***
Parental Marital Status					
Separated or Divorced	8	9.0	45	43.7	
Intact	81	91.0	58	56.3	28.77***

***p < .001.

Significant group differences also were evident for parental marital stability. Latina/o households revealed greater marital dysfunction than Southeast Asian households did (44% vs. 9%, respectively). Table 7-5 reveals that Latina/o respondents' parents were more likely to be separated or divorced than the Southeast Asian participants' parents, X^2 (1, 192) = 28.77, p < .001.

In sum, the Southeast Asian families were both more likely to be an immigrant sample and to be impoverished, but they were still more likely to advanced in grade. The Latinas/os were more likely to be in college preparatory courses, and their level of parental marital instability was greater.

Between-Group Comparisons

A multivariate analysis of variance (MANOVA) was conducted to determine whether there were overall group differences for the bicultural competence indices (CBCS). The univariate F for each of the bicultural competence indices were examined separately. Contrary to the hypothesis, Table 7-6 below reveals that there was a significant group difference for the CBCS-language dimension, F (1, 192) = 5.56, p < .05, in favor of the Latinas/os (Latinas/os: M = 4.20; Southeast Asian: M = 3.87) but not for the CBCS-identity/values dimension. Further, gender differences for the bicultural competence indices also were explored; however, no significant gender differences on these indices were found.

Table 7-6. Mean CBCS Indices Scores

Index	Group		Multivariate	
	Southeast Asian (n = 89)	Latina/o (n = 103)	F	df
CBCS-Language Dimension				
M	3.87	4.20		
SD	1.06	0.93	5.56*	1
Covarying generation status:				
M	3.81	4.25		
SD	0.11	0.11	7.24**	1

Covarying generation & SES:

M	3.92	4.15		
SD	0.12	0.11	1.47	1

CBCS-Identity/Values Dimension

M	3.48	3.70		
SD	1.79	1.68	0.74	1

*p < .05. **p < .01.

Since the groups were significantly different in terms of generational status (see above and Table 7-1), a MANCOVA was conducted with generational status as a covariate. The univariate F statistic was examined separately for each of the indices. Table 7-6 also reveals that this pattern strengthened as a result of controlling for generational status. A greater group differences was found again in favor of the Latina/o group for the CBCS-language dimension, F (1, 192) = 7.24, p < .01 (note: no difference for the CBCS-identity/values dimension). The Latina/o group reported better maintenance of bicultural competence in language as evidenced by their grater score overall (Latinas/os: M = 4.20; Southeast Asians: M = 3.86), regardless of generational status. However, both groups appeared to be equally effective at maintaining bicultural competence in identity and values (Latinas/os: M = 3.70; Southeast Asians: M = 3.48).

Since the groups were found to differ markedly on SES, with the Latina/o group reporting a much higher SES level than the Southeast Asian respondents did, a MANCOVA was conducted with both generational status and SES as covariates. As mentioned in Chapter 3, LaFromboise, Coleman, and Gerton (1993) concluded that socioeconomic status might be a significant factor influencing an individual's ability to develop and refine the necessary skills for bicultural competence. Indeed, this group difference disappeared after controlling for SES (see Table 7-6).

In sum, Latina/o and Southeast Asian subjects were hypothesized to not differ in bicultural competence. The results of these analyses supported this hypothesis only when controlling for SES. This finding adds credence to LaFromboise et al.'s conclusions of the importance of SES in the development of bicultural competence.

Students reported on a recent stressful event across the familial and academic contexts. Latina/o and Southeast Asian subjects were hypothesized to not differ in the types of stressors reported on across contexts. Contrary to the hypothesis, Table 7-7 below reveals that for the familial stressor, the Southeast Asian students were more likely to report minor problems (minor problem: 37%, work/school: 14%) than the Latina/o students (minor problem: 27%; work/school: 6%). The Latinas/os were more likely to report major problems (loss: 22%; major problems: 26%) than the Southeast Asian students (loss: 15%; major problems: 20%) for the familial stressor, X^2 (4, 186) = 7.19, p < .05.

Table 7-7. Comparisons of Stressors across Ethnic Groups

Group Stressor	Southeast Asian (n = 89)		Latina/o (n = 103)		
	n	%	n	%	X^2
Familial Stressor					
Minor problem	32	37.2	27	27.0	
Work/school	12	14.0	6	6.0	
Relational	12	14.0	19	19.0	
Loss	13	15.1	22	22.0	
Major problem	17	19.8	26	26.0	7.19*
Academic Stressor					
Minor problem	34	39.1	35	35.4	
Work/school	28	32.2	34	34.3	
Relational	16	18.4	16	16.2	
Loss	2	2.3	2	2.0	
Major problem	7	8.0	12	12.1	1.14

*p < .05.

A cross-context comparison was conducted to determine whether stressors differed as a function of context. Table 7-8 reveals that there were significant differences in stressors across contexts, X^2 (4, 186) = 18.45, p < .001. Respondents were more likely to report minor problems than major problems in the academic context, while in the familial context respondents were equally likely to report both minor and major problems.

Table 7-8. Comparisons of Stressors across Contexts
Familial Context Stressors   Minor Prob.   Work/School
Relational   Loss   Major Prob.

	n	%	n	%	n	%	n	%	n	%
Academic Context										
Minor Prob.	27	14.9	16	8.8	13	7.2	1	0.6	1	0.6
Work/School	3	1.7	6	3.3	4	2.2	1	0.6	3	1.7
Relational	9	5.0	12	6.6	5	2.8	-	-	4	2.2
Loss	12	6.6	12	6.6	4	2.2	2	1.1	5	2.8
Major Prob.	15	8.3	15	8.3	5	2.8	-	-	6	3.3
Total	66	36.5	61	33.6	31	17.2	4	2.3	19	10.6

$X^2(16, 181) = 18.45***$

***$p < .001$.

Not surprisingly, Latina/o students reported greater stress in the familial context ($M = 5.20$) than the Southeast Asian youth ($M = 4.45$), multivariate $F(1, 186) = 5.55$, $p < .05$ (see Table 7-9 below). Latina/o subjects were more likely to report both major problems (see above) and greater stress in the familial context than Southeast Asian youth, which is interesting because Latina/o and Southeast Asian subjects were hypothesized to not differ on these indices. However, as hypothesized, the groups were indistinguishable regarding both academic stressors (see above) and academic stress ratings (also see Table 7-9). Gender differences for the stress ratings also were explored; however, no significant gender differences on these indices were found. Finally, Table 7-10 below reveals that there were no significant differences in stress ratings as a function of context.

Table 7-9. Mean Stress Scores across Ethnic Groups

Group Multivariate Item	Southeast Asian ($\underline{n} = 89$)	Latina/o ($\underline{n} = 103$)	$\underline{F}(1, 180)$
Familial Stress Rating			
$\underline{M}$	4.41	5.26	
$\underline{SD}$	1.74	1.73	10.67***
Academic Stress Rating			
$\underline{M}$	4.47	4.73	
$\underline{SD}$	1.80	1.87	.91

***$\underline{p} < .001$.

Table 7-10. Mean Stress and Coping Processes across Contexts Scores

Item	Context Familial	Academic	$\underline{t}$
Stress Rating			
$\underline{M}$	4.87	4.61	
$\underline{SD}$	1.78	1.83	1.62
Direct Action Coping			
$\underline{M}$	1.73	1.86	
$\underline{SD}$	1.11	1.08	-1.23
Social Support Coping			
$\underline{M}$	1.46	1.31	
$\underline{SD}$	1.19	1.16	1.51
Coping Efficacy			
$\underline{M}$	2.94	3.10	
$\underline{SD}$	1.03	1.07	-1.60

Regarding the appraisal process, Table 7-11 below reveals that there were no significant group differences in appraising stress as a challenge in both the familial and academic contexts as hypothesized. Table 7-12 below reveals that both groups were more likely to appraise stress as a challenge in the academic context than in the familial context, $X^2(1, 186) = 6.08$, $p < .05$. In sum, both groups did not appear to appraise the familial situation as a challenge, and they did not differ in challenge stress appraisals across contexts.

Table 7-11.
Comparisons of Stress Appraisals as Challenge across Ethnic Groups

Challenge	Group Southeast Asian (n =89)		Latina/o (n = 103)		
	n	%	n	%	X^2
Familial Context					
yes	13	15.1	21	21.0	
no	73	84.9	79	79.0	1.07
Academic Context					
yes	35	40.2	38	38.4	
no	52	59.8	61	61.6	0.07

Table 7-12. Comparisons of Stress Appraisals as
Challenge across Contexts

Challenge Appraisals	Familial Context			
	Yes		No	
	n	%	n	%
Academic Context				
Yes	19	10.5	51	28.2
No	14	7.7	97	53.6
Total	33	18.2	148	81.8

$X^2(1, 181) = 6.08*$ $*p < .05.$

Regarding coping and coping efficacy, Table 7-13 below reveals that there were also no significant group differences in social support coping, direct action coping, and coping efficacy across contexts, as hypothesized. Gender differences for these indices also were explored.

Table 7-13. Mean Coping and Efficacy Scores across Ethnic Groups

Item	Group		Multivariate
	Southeast Asian (n = 89)	Latina/o (n = 103)	$F(1, 180)$
Familial Social Support Coping			
M	1.39	1.53	
SD	1.17	1.22	.62
Academic Direct Action Coping			
M	1.71	1.98	
SD	1.13	1.03	2.77
Familial Coping Efficacy			
M	3.02	2.88	
SD	0.94	1.11	.91
Academic Coping Efficacy			
M	3.06	3.13	
SD	0.94	1.18	.21

Gender differences on these indices were found only for social support coping in the familial context. Table 7-14 below reveals that both Southeast Asian females (M = 1.55) and Latina females (M = 1.64) reported greater social support coping in the familial context than Southeast Asian males (M = 1.15) and Latino males (M = 1.26), multivariate F(1, 186) = 6.86, p < .05. Table 7-10 above reveals that there were no significant differences in coping and coping efficacy as a function of context.

Table 7-14.
Mean Familial Social Support Coping Scores by Gender

Group	Gender Female	Male	Multivariate F (1, 186)
Southeast Asian			
M	1.55	1.15	
SD	1.17	1.08	
Latina/o			
M	1.64	1.26	
SD	1.24	1.11	6.86*

*p < .05.

In sum, coping and coping efficacy did not differ as a function of ethnicity, gender, and context with the exception of social support coping, which only differed as a function of gender. Further, Latina/o and Southeast Asian youth were hypothesized to not differ in stress and coping processes across contexts; however, significant group differences were found for types of stress and stress ratings in the familial context. Latina/o subjects were more likely to report greater marital instability, major problems, and greater stress in the familial context than the Southeast Asian youth.

The means (Ms) and standard deviations (SDs) for the exploratory variables of self-esteem and depressed mood are presented in Table 7-15 below for each ethnic group. As hypothesized, the groups did not differ in self-esteem or in depressed mood, despite the greater discord in the Latina/o families. Gender differences for these indices also were explored; however, no significant gender differences on these indices were found.

Table 7-15.
Mean Adaptive Processes Scores

Scale	Group		
	Southeast Asian ($\underline{n}$ = 89)	Latina/o ($\underline{n}$ = 103)	$\underline{t}$
Self-esteem			
$\underline{M}$	23.00	22.60	
$\underline{SD}$	3.95	4.19	0.67
Depressed Mood			
$\underline{M}$	8.28	8.49	
$\underline{SD}$	3.91	4.28	-0.34

The means (Ms) and standard deviations (SDs) for GPA and the exploratory variable of academic goals are presented in Table 7-16 below for each ethnic group. Contrary to the hypotheses that there would be no significant group differences on these indices, Table 7-16 also reveals that the groups differed significantly on GPA and academic goals in favor of the Southeast Asian group; GPA: $\underline{t}(192) = 5.41$, $\underline{p} < .001$; academic goals: $\underline{t}(192) = 2.07$, $\underline{p} < .05$. Despite the Southeast Asian subjects' immigrant status and lower SES, they still managed to reveal higher GPA and academic goals as evidenced by their greater scores overall (Southeast Asians' GPA: $\underline{M} = 2.96$; Latinas/os' GPA: $\underline{M} = 2.23$; Southeast Asians' academic goals: $\underline{M} = 59.05$; Latinas/os' academic goals: $\underline{M} = 56.63$).

Table 7-16. Mean Academic Scores

Scale/Item	Group Southeast Asian (n = 89)	Latina/o (n = 103)	t
GPA			
M	2.96	2.23	
SD	0.90	0.97	5.41***
Academic Goals			
M	59.05	56.63	
SD	7.61	8.46	2.07*

*p < .05. ***p < .001.

Gender differences for these indices also were explored herein. Gender differences on these indices were found only for GPA. Table 7-17 below reveals that both Southeast Asian females ($\underline{M}$ = 3.14) and Latina females ($\underline{M}$ = 2.31) revealed higher GPAs than their male counterparts (Southeast Asian: $\underline{M}$ = 2.67; Latino: $\underline{M}$ = 2.12), multivariate $\underline{F}(1, 192) = 3.04$, p < .05.

Table 7-17. Mean GPA Scores by Gender

Group	Gender Female	Male	Multivariate F (1, 192)
Southeast Asian			
M	3.14	2.67	
SD	0.85	0.91	
Latina/o			
M	2.31	2.12	
SD	0.97	0.97	3.04*

*p < .05.

The means (Ms) and standard deviations (SDs) for the exploratory variables of perceived parental warmth and perceived school discrimination are presented for each group in Table 7-18 below. As hypothesized, the groups also did not differ significantly in perceptions of parental warmth and school discrimination. Interestingly, the Latinas/os did not score lower on perceptions of parental warmth, despite the greater discord in the Latina/o families. Gender differences for these indices also were explored herein; however, no significant gender differences on these indices were found.

Table 7-18. Mean Environmental Factors Scores

| Environmental Factor | Group | | t |
	Southeast Asian (n = 89)	Latina/o (n = 103)	
Perceived Parental Warmth			
M	27.98	26.50	
SD	6.10	6.22	1.65
Perceived School Discrimination			
M	11.49	12.08	
SD	3.67	4.76	-0.94

In conjunction, the between-groups comparisons conducted herein partially supported the primary hypotheses of the study, namely the null hypotheses. The groups were hypothesized to not differ significantly on the aforementioned variables. Indeed, the groups of study did not differ significantly on most of the measures. No differences were found for the bicultural competence indices when controlling for SES, most of the stress and coping processes across contexts indices, depressed mood, self-esteem, perceived parental warmth, and perceived school discrimination.

Interestingly, they did differ, however, on some of the indices under investigation, namely on stressors and stress ratings in the familial context, GPA, and academic goals. On the one hand, the findings reveal that the Latina/o group was more likely to experience greater stress in the familial context (i.e., greater parental marital dysfunction, more severe stressors, and greater stress ratings). On the other hand, the Southeast Asian group was more likely to be an immigrant sample with a lower SES level, but was more likely to reveal greater grade advancement, a higher GPA, and higher academic goals. Lastly, females were more likely to use social support coping in the familial context and had a higher GPA than males.

Within-Group Analyses

In this section, within-group patterns for the correlations among the bicultural competence indices, stress and coping processes across contexts, depressed mood, self-esteem, GPA, academic goals, perceived parental warmth, and perceived school discrimination were discussed for the combined ethnic sample ($\underline{N}$ = 192). Second, within-group patterns also were examined separately for each ethnic group (i.e., Latina/o and Southeast Asian) to determine whether there were any significant differences in these patterns as a function of ethnicity.

Regarding the relationships among bicultural competence and stress and coping processes across contexts, it was expected that bicultural competence would be negatively associated with stress ratings across contexts. Contrary to the hypothesis, there was a marginally positive relationship, rather than a negative correlation, between the CBCS-identity/values dimension and familial stress ratings, $\underline{r}$ = .14, $\underline{p}$ < .06 (see Table 7-19 below). The relationship between the CBCS-language dimension and familial stress ratings did not approach significance, however. Interestingly, the CBCS-language and identity/values dimensions were not associated significantly with academic stress ratings, nor were the CBCS dimensions associated with challenge stress appraisals.

Table 7-19: Combined Ethnic Sample (N = 192) Correlations among the Bicultural Competence, Stress and Coping Processes across Contexts, Adaptive Processes, and Academic Variables

Variable	2	3	4	5	6	7	8	9	10	11	12	13	14
1. CBCS-language	.35**	.11	.12	.09	.11	-.05	-.01	.07	-.02	.23**	-.11	.28**	.06
2. CBCS-identity/values		.14	.04	.15*	.17*	.01	-.03	.23**	.09	.25**	-.20**	.24**	.01
3. Familial Stress			-.06	.13	-.17*	.31**	-.11	.11	.03	-.02	.23**	-.02	-.06
4. Familial Challenge Appraisals				.08	-.07	-.13	.17*	-.08	-.02	.15*	-.14*	.03	-.09
5. Familial Social Support Coping					.08	.09	-.05	.02	.21**	.04	.04	.04	.05
6. Familial Coping Efficacy						-.01	.01	.01	.01	.23**	.28**	-.15*	.19**
7. Academic Stress							-.01	-.10	.29**	-.13	.30**	-.16*	-.01
8. Academic Challenge Appraisals								-.01	-.11	.01	-.02	-.04	.01
9. Academic Direct Action Coping									.11	.12	-.04	.19**	-.01
10. Academic Coping Efficacy										.19**	-.08	.07	-.05
11. Self-esteem											-.53**	.18*	.25**
12. Depressed Mood												-.12	-.15*
13. Academic Goals													.22**
14. GPA													

*p < .05. **p < .01.

Regarding the relationships among bicultural competence and the coping responses, Table 7-19 above also reveals that there were positive associations between the CBCS-identity/values dimension and familial social support coping, r = .15, p < .05, and academic direct action coping, r = .23, p < .01. Table 7-19 also reveals that there was a positive relationship between the CBCS-identity/values dimension and familial efficacy, r = .17, p < .05.

In sum, bicultural competence in identity/values appears to be somewhat related to only familial stress, not academic stress, to both direct action coping in the academic context and social support coping in the familial context, and to familial coping efficacy. Interestingly, bicultural competence in language was not significantly associated with any of the stress and coping processes across contexts variables. It appears that bicultural competence, specifically in identity and values, is related to stress and coping processes across contexts.

Regarding the relationship between bicultural competence and the adaptive processes variables, Table 7-19 also reveals that there were positive associations between the bicultural competence indices and self-esteem: language: r = .23, p < .01; identity/values: r = .25, p < .01. Further, only the CBCS-identity/values dimension was related to depressed mood in the expected direction, r = -.20, p < .01. It appears that bicultural competence is related to a number of adaptive processes, namely greater self-esteem and lower depressed mood.

The correlations between bicultural competence and the academic variables reveal that only academic goals was correlated significantly with the two bicultural competence indices. Interestingly, GPA did not correlate with bicultural competence (see Table 7-19). Table 7-19 reveals that there were positive associations between the bicultural competence indices and academic goals; language: r = .28, p < .01; identity/values: r = .24, p < .01. It seems that bicultural competence is related to academic goals but not to GPA.

In sum, the CBCS identity/values dimension was more strongly associated with the other variables than was the language dimension. The CBCS identity/values dimension was positively correlated with direct action coping in the academic context and social support coping in the familial context, as well as coping efficacy. It was also positively correlated with self-esteem and academic goals, and negatively associated with depressed mood, but was not associated directly with GPA.

It was expected that bicultural competence would be related to lower stress ratings and challenge stress appraisals across contexts (i.e., familial and academic), which in turn would be associated with both social support coping in the familial context and direct action coping in the academic context. Stress ratings were hypothesized to be inversely associated with challenge stress appraisals and coping across contexts. Contrary to the hypotheses, Table 7-19 above also reveals that familial stress was not significantly associated with challenge stress appraisals, direct action coping, or social support coping across contexts. However, academic stress was positively associated with only direct action coping in the same context, $r = .29$, $p < .01$. In sum, stress ratings were not associated with challenge stress appraisals, which in turn were not associated with coping across contexts. Stress ratings, however, were associated with direct action coping but only in the academic context.

Social support coping in the familial context and direct action coping in the academic context were expected to be associated with coping efficacy across contexts. A positive association was hypothesized between these coping responses and coping efficacy. Contrary to the hypothesis, Table 7-19 also reveals that social support coping in the familial context was not significantly associated with coping efficacy in this context. Also, contrary to the hypothesis, Table 7-19 also reveals that direct action coping in the academic context was not significantly associated with coping efficacy in this context.

It was expected that coping efficacy across contexts would be related to a number of adaptive outcomes; these are greater self-esteem and lower depressed mood. Positive associations were hypothesized amongst coping efficacy across contexts and self-esteem (i.e., the greater the coping efficacy across contexts, the greater the self-esteem), whereas inverse associations were hypothesized amongst coping efficacy across contexts and depressed mood (i.e., the greater the coping efficacy across contexts, the lower the depressed mood). As hypothesized, Table 7-19 also reveals that familial coping efficacy was positively associated with self-esteem, $r = .28$, $p < .01$, and inversely associated with depressed mood, $r = -.15$, $p < .05$. Interestingly, academic coping efficacy was only associated with self-esteem, not depressed mood. Further, Table 7-19 reveals that academic coping efficacy was positively associated with self-esteem, r = .19, p < .05. In sum, it appears that coping efficacy across contexts is related to the adaptive processes of self-esteem and low depressed mood.

It was expected that coping efficacy across contexts also would be related to a number of academic outcomes; these are GPA and the exploratory variable of academic goals. Positive associations were hypothesized amongst coping efficacy across contexts and GPA (i.e., the greater the coping efficacy across contexts, the higher the GPA). Coping efficacy across contexts also was hypothesized to be positively correlated with academic goals (i.e., the greater the coping efficacy across contexts, the higher the academic goals). Interestingly, only familial coping efficacy was positively associated with both GPA, r = .19, p < .01, and academic goals, r = .19, p < .01 (see Table 7-19 above).

Regarding the exploratory relationships amongst the adaptive processes variables and the academic variables, Table 7-19 reveals that self-esteem was positively associated with both GPA, r = .25, p < .01, and academic goals, r = .18, p < .05, whereas depressed mood was inversely associated with GPA, r = -.15, p < .05, but not with academic goals. Lastly, regarding the exploratory relationship between academic goals and GPA, Table 7-19 also reveals that academic goals was positively associated with GPA, r = .22, p < .01.

Regarding the relationships among the exploratory environmental variables (e.g., perceived parental warmth), the adaptive processes variables (e.g., self-esteem), and the academic variables (i.e., GPA and the exploratory academic goals variable), Table 7-20 below reveals that perceived parental warmth was positively associated with self-esteem, r = .40, p < .01, inversely associated with depressed mood, r = -.42, p < .01, positively associated with academic goals, r = .39, p < .01, but not associated with GPA.

Table 7-20: Combined Ethnic Sample (N = 192)
Correlations among the Environmental Factors, Adaptive Processes,
and Academic Variables

Variable	2	3	4	5	6
1. Perceived Parental Warmth	.02	.40**	-.42**	.39**	.09
2. Perceived School Discrimination		-.32**	.34**	.05	-.28**
3. Self-esteem			.53**	.18*	.25**
4. Depressed Mood				-.12	-.15*
5. Academic Goals					.22**
6. GPA					

*p < .05. **p < .01.

On the other hand, Table 7-20 above also reveals that perceived school discrimination was inversely associated with self-esteem, $r = -.32$, $p < .01$, positively associated with depressed mood, $r = .34$, $p < .01$, and inversely associated with GPA, $r = -.28$, $p < .01$, but not associated with academic goals.

Lastly, correlation matrices were generated separately for each ethnic group to determine whether there were any significant differences in these patterns as a function of ethnicity. Between-group comparisons of the correlations reveal that the matrices were indeed similar, but differed slightly in the following ways (see Tables 7-21 to 7-24 below).

Table 7-21: Southeast Asian (n = 89) Correlations among the Bicultural Competence, Stress and Coping Processes across Contexts, Adaptive Processes, and Academic Variables

Variable	2	3	4	5	6	7	8	9	10	11	12	13	14
1. CBCS-language	.43**	.24**	-.10	.39**	.15*	.13	.13	.12	.18*	-.02	.01	.10	.08
2. CBCS-identity/values		.29**	-.40**	.34**	-.04	.09	.09	.10	.12	-.02	-.04	.37**	.24**
3. Familial Stress			-.00	-.03	.00	.37**	-.17*	.16*	.07	.12	.09	.03	.11
4. Familial Challenge Appraisals				.06	-.13	-.09	.12	-.07	.04	.09	-.17*	.04	-.08
5. Familial Social Support Coping					-.01	-.05	-.11	.13	-.19**	.07	.05	.06	.14
6. Familial Coping Efficacy						-.02	.07	-.07	.16*	.25**	-.07	.22**	.23**
7. Academic Stress							-.10	.28**	-.05	-.12	.14	-.01	.10
8. Academic Challenge Appraisals								-.17*	.07	-.12	-.02	.04	.01
9. Academic Direct Action Coping									.24**	.23**	-.27**	.26**	.07
10. Academic Coping Efficacy										.21**	-.17*	.13	.01
11. Self-esteem											-.44**	.30**	.22**
12. Depressed Mood												-.35**	.05
13. Academic Goals													.22**
14. GPA													

*p < .05. **p < .01.

Table 7-22: Latina/o (n = 103) Correlations among the Bicultural Competence, Stress and Coping Processes across Contexts, Adaptive Processes, and Academic Variables

Variable	2	3	4	5	6	7	8	9	10	11	12	13	14
1. CBCS-language	.25**	.24**	-.14	.24**	.11	.02	.16*	.04	.08	-.11	.01	-.01	-.12
2. CBCS-identity/values		.22**	-.03	.19**	.09	.16*	.01	.17*	.23**	.03	-.01	.07	.02
3. Familial Stress			-.07	.25**	-.27**	.16*	.26**	-.06	.03	-.02	-.11	.35**	-.05
4. Familial Challenge Appraisals				.11	-.03	-.16*	.23**	-.06	-.05	.19**	-.13	.03	-.16*
5. Familial Social Support Coping					.17*	-.05	.15*	.28**	.18*	.03	.12	-.11	.03
6. Familial Coping Efficacy						.00	-.03	.10	.28**	.29**	-.20**	.16*	.14
7. Academic Stress							-.11	.29**	-.18*	-.19**	.43**	.22**	-.05
8. Academic Challenge Appraisals								-.06	-.03	.07	-.05	.07	.03
9. Academic Direct Action Coping									.01	.02	.15*	.15*	-.00
10. Academic Coping Efficacy										.17*	-.01	.03	-.01
11. Self-esteem											-.59**	.08	.27**
12. Depressed Mood												.04	-.29**
13. Academic Goals													.15*
14. GPA													

*p < .05. **p < .01

Table 7-23: Southeast Asian (n = 89) Correlations among the
Environmental Factors, Adaptive Processes, and Academic Variables

Variable	2	3	4	5	6
1. Perceived Parental Warmth	-.01	.33**	-.45**	.51**	.05
2. Perceived School Discrimination	-.33**		.29**	-.02	-.09
3. Self-esteem		-.44**		.30**	.22**
4. Depressed Mood			-.35**		.05
5. Academic Goals				.22**	
6. GPA					

**p < .01.

Table 7-24: Latina/o (n = 103) Correlations among the Environmental
Factors, Adaptive Processes, and Academic Variables

Variable	2	3	4	5	6
1. Perceived Parental Warmth	.05	.44**	-.36**	.29**	.03
2. Perceived School Discrimination	-.31**		.37**	.10	-.38**
3. Self-esteem		-.59**		.08	.27**
4. Depressed Mood			.04	-.29**	
5. Academic Goals				.15*	
6. GPA					

*p < .05. **p < .01.

Bicultural competence was more strongly (inversely) associated
with depressed mood and academic coping processes for the Southeast
Asians. On the other hand, bicultural competence was more strongly
associated with familial stress and coping processes for the Latinas/os.
Self-esteem was more strongly correlated with academic goals and
academic direct action coping for the Southeast Asians. On the other
hand, self-esteem was more strongly associated with familial challenge
appraisals and academic stress for the Latinas/os. Depressed mood was
more strongly correlated (inversely) with academic goals, academic

direct action coping, and academic coping efficacy for the Southeast Asians. On the other hand, depressed mood was more strongly correlated with GPA, familial stress, familial coping efficacy, and academic stress for the Latinas/os.

Further, academic goals were more strongly correlated with academic stress for the Latinas/os, whereas academic goals were more strongly associated with academic direct action coping for the Southeast Asians. GPA was more strongly correlated with familial challenge appraisals for the Latinas/os, whereas GPA was more strongly associated with familial coping efficacy for the Southeast Asians. Familial stress was more strongly correlated with familial social support coping and familial coping efficacy for the Latinas/os, whereas familial stress was more strongly associated with academic challenge appraisals and academic direct action coping for the Southeast Asians.

Familial challenge appraisals were more strongly correlated with academic stress and academic challenge appraisals for the Latinas/os. Familial social support coping was more strongly correlated with familial coping efficacy, academic challenge appraisals, and academic direct action coping for the Latinas/os. Academic stress was more strongly associated with academic coping efficacy for the Latinas/os. Academic challenge appraisals were more strongly correlated with academic direct action coping for the Southeast Asians. Academic direct action coping was more strongly associated with academic coping efficacy for the Southeast Asians. Lastly, perceived school discrimination was more strongly correlated (inversely) with GPA for the Latinas/os.

In sum, the expected relationships amongst bicultural competence, stress and coping processes across contexts, adaptive processes, and academic variables were not entirely confirmed in this study. Interestingly, the expected relationships were more evident in the familial context than in the academic context. The familial context appears to be more salient for the sample of study.

A possible explanation for the lack of support for the expected relationships could be attributable to the fact that each coping strategy (i.e., direct action coping and social support coping) on the Measure of Daily Coping was assessed with only one item and thus, was unable to account for enough of the variance. For this reason, alternative study models, which utilized different configurations of the variables of interest also were conducted. Further, an exploratory model was generated to determine whether this model provided a better explanation of the research findings.

The following structural equation models were constructed: (1) the original study model, which is depicted as a composite model in Figure 7-1; (2) a bicultural competence, familial stress and coping processes, alternative study model; (3) a bicultural competence, academic stress and coping processes, alternative study model; and (4) an environmental factors exploratory model. The models are described further below.

Structural Equation Models

According to the original study model, bicultural competence was hypothesized to be related to lower stress ratings and greater likelihood of appraising stress as a challenge across the familial and academic domains, which in turn was expected to be related to greater social support coping in the familial context and greater direct action coping in the academic context. Social support coping in the familial context and direct action coping in the academic context were hypothesized to be related to greater coping efficacy across contexts, which in turn was expected to be related to greater self-esteem, lower depressed mood, and greater academic resilience (i.e., GPA).

To determine the validity of this model, two latent variable, structural equation analyses, utilizing Amos, Version 4.0 (Arbuckle, 1994-99), were conducted separately for each context for sake of simplicity on the combined ethnic sample ($\underline{N}$ = 192) (see Figure 7-1 below). Since the ethnic specific correlation matrices were similar and the Southeast Asian group lacked sufficient power ($\underline{n}$ = 89), separate structural equation analyses for each ethnic group were not conducted. Contrary to the hypotheses, these models indicated a poor fit, evident by inflated chi-square values (e.g., academic context: $\underline{X}^2$ = 133.83, $\underline{df}$ = 27).

Figure 7-1: Bicultural Competence, Stress and Coping Processes across Contexts, Original Study Model

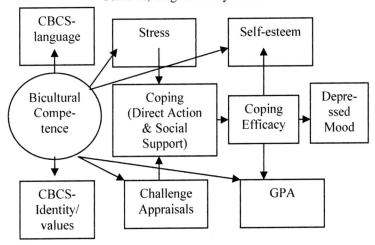

Since the original study models were not supported, alternative study models were developed, which explored the variables of interest in different configurations. Two latent variables, structural equation analyses also were conducted separately for each context (i.e., familial and academic) for sake of simplicity. The bicultural competence, familial stress and coping processes, alternative study model will be discussed first.

The correlation matrix (Table 7-19 above) was utilized to guide the selection and placement of the variables in the model. This alternative study model differed from the original study model in the following ways. Since bicultural competence did not correlate with stress ratings across contexts, stress was utilized as an independent or exogenous variable in this alternative study model. Second, both direct and indirect effects of all variables were examined in this model. Third, appraisals of stress across contexts and depressed mood were eliminated because the fit indices indicated a poor fit of this model with these variables.

Figure 7-2 below provides the standardized maximum likelihood estimates of the model for the combined ethnic sample ($\underline{N}$ = 192). To control for the influence of other factors on the variables of interest, a number of error terms were incorporated into the model. The first indicator (i.e., CBCS-language dimension) of the latent variable (bicultural competence) was fixed at 1.0. The CBCS-language and identity/values dimensions both significantly loaded onto the latent construct of bicultural competence. Figure 7-2 reveals that the loadings were reasonably high, ranging from .53 to .66, indicating acceptable reliability for these indicators. Table 7-25 reveals the standardized indirect, direct, and total effects for this model.

Figure 7-2: Bicultural Competence, Familial Stress and Coping Processes, Alternative Study Model (N = 192)

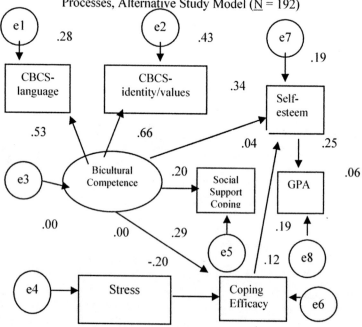

Chi-square = 13.618, df = 13, p = .401. RMSEA = .016. CFI = .992. RFI = .771.

The first step in the original study model proposed that bicultural competence is inversely associated with stress ratings and positively associated with challenge stress appraisals across contexts. In other words, the greater the bicultural competence, the lower the stress ratings and the greater likelihood of appraising stress as a challenge across contexts. Turning to the standardized structural coefficients of this alternative study model, surprisingly, Figure 7-2 above reveals that the construct of bicultural competence was positively and significantly related to self-esteem (beta = .34), familial social support coping (beta = .20), and familial coping efficacy (beta = .29) but not to familial stress ratings.

The second step of the original study model proposed that stress ratings and challenge stress appraisals are associated with social support coping in the familial context. In other words, lower stress ratings and greater likelihood of appraising stress as a challenge were hypothesized to be related to greater social support coping in the familial context. Contrary to the hypotheses, stress ratings were not related to social support coping in the familial context, but they were inversely and significantly related to coping efficacy (beta = -.20) (see Figure 7-2 above).

The final steps of the original study model proposed that social support coping is positively associated with coping efficacy in the familial context, which in turn is associated with a number of adaptive outcomes. Interestingly, stress ratings, rather than social support coping, were associated with coping efficacy in the familial context. Social support coping was not significantly related to stress, coping efficacy, self-esteem, or GPA. As expected, Figure 7-2 above reveals that familial coping efficacy was positively and significantly related to self-esteem (beta = .19) but not to GPA. Contrary to the hypothesis, self-esteem, not coping efficacy, was positively and significantly related to GPA (beta = .25).

As shown in Figure 7-2 above, there is a strong fit of this model to the data, in that the chi-square value of 13.62 is not statistically significant (p = .40). The Root Mean Square Error of Approximation (RMSEA) of .02, the Comparative Fit Index (CFI) of .99, and the Relative Fit Index (RFI) of .77, all support the conclusion that the model fits the data reasonably well.

Table 7-25 below reveals that a direct effect of bicultural competence on GPA was not significant.   Although bicultural competence did not have direct effects on GPA, there was a slight tendency towards an indirect effect of bicultural competence on GPA via familial coping efficacy and self-esteem. Table 7-25 reveals that the primary pathways to GPA are through familial coping efficacy and self-esteem.   In sum, the findings relating bicultural competence to GPA were not entirely confirmed in this study. However, the findings provide important evidence linking bicultural competence to coping processes, self-esteem, and GPA.

Table 7-25. Combined Ethnic Sample (N = 192) Standardized Indirect/Direct/Total Effects of Bicultural Competence, Familial Stress and Coping Processes, and Self-esteem on GPA

Variable	Indirect		Direct	Total
Bicultural Competence	.09	. . .	.09	
Stress	.01**	. . .	.01**	
Coping Efficacy	.05*	. . .	.05*	
Self-esteem	. . .	.25	.25	

*$p < .05$. **$p < .01$.

Figure 7-3 below depicts the second alternative study model for the academic context. The correlation matrix (Table 7-19 above) also was utilized to guide the selection and placement of the variables in the model. This alternative study model also differed from the original study model in the following ways.   Since bicultural competence did not correlate with stress ratings across contexts, stress also was utilized as an independent or exogenous variable in this alternative study model. Second, both direct and indirect effects of all variables also were examined in this model.   Third, appraisals of stress across contexts and depressed mood were eliminated because the fit indices also indicated a poor fit of this model with these variables.

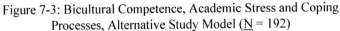

Figure 7-3: Bicultural Competence, Academic Stress and Coping
Processes, Alternative Study Model (N = 192)

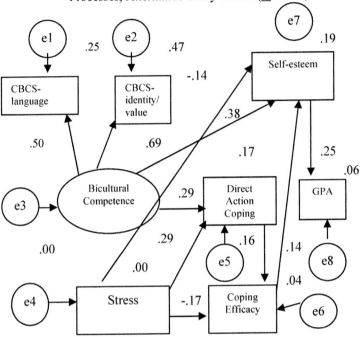

Chi-square = 7.757, df = 11, p = .735. RMSEA = .000. CFI = 1.000.
RFI = .994.

Figure 7-3 above provides the standardized maximum likelihood estimates of this alternative study model for the combined ethnic sample. The variance of "error3" (i.e., e3) was set at "1.0" to deal with a negative variance estimate. The negative error variance disappeared as a result of this procedure. As in the previous model, the CBCS-language and identity/values dimensions both significantly loaded onto the latent construct of bicultural competence. Figure 7-3 reveals that the loadings were reasonably high, ranging from .50 to .69, indicating acceptable reliability for these indicators. Table 7-26 below reveals the standardized indirect, direct, and total effects for this model.

Table 7-26. Combined Ethnic Sample (N = 192) Standardized
Indirect/Direct/Total Effects of Bicultural Competence, Academic
Stress and Coping Processes, and Self-esteem on GPA

Variable	Indirect	Direct	Total
Bicultural Competence	.08	. . .	.08
Stress	.04*	. . .	.04*
Direct Action Coping	.01**	. . .	.01**
Coping Efficacy	.04*	. . .	.04*
Self-esteem	. . .	.25	.25

*p < .05. **p < .01.

To recapitulate, the first step in the original study model proposed
that bicultural competence is inversely associated with stress ratings
and positively associated with challenge stress appraisals. In other
words, the greater the bicultural competence, the lower the stress
ratings and the greater the likelihood of appraising stress as a challenge
across contexts. Contrary to the hypotheses, bicultural competence was
not related to academic stress, but it was positively and significantly
related to direct action coping (beta = .29) and to self-esteem (beta =
.38) (see Figure 7-3 above).

The second step of the original study model proposed that stress
ratings and challenge stress appraisals are associated with direct action
coping in the academic context. In other words, lower stress ratings
and greater likelihood of appraising stress as a challenge were
hypothesized to be related to greater direct action coping in the
academic context. Figure 7-3 above also reveals that rather than a
negative association, academic stress ratings were positively and
significantly related to academic direct action coping (beta = .29) and
inversely associated with both academic coping efficacy (beta = -.17)
and self-esteem (beta = -.14).

The final steps of the original study model proposed that academic direct action coping is positively associated with coping efficacy, which in turn is associated with a number of adaptive outcomes. As expected, direct action coping was positively and significantly related to coping efficacy in the academic context (beta = .16), which in turn was positively and marginally related to only self-esteem (beta = .14) but not to GPA. Lastly, self-esteem was positively and significantly related to GPA (beta = .25).

As shown in Figure 7-3 above, there is an acceptable fit of this model to the data, in that the chi-square value of 7.76 is not statistically significant (p = .74). The Root Mean Square Error of Approximation (RMSEA) of .00, the Comparative Fit Index (CFI) of 1.00, and the Relative Fit Index (RFI) of .99, all support the conclusion that this model also fits the data very well.

In sum, as in the previous alternative study model, bicultural competence was expected to be related to academic resilience (i.e., GPA) via the mediating variables of stress and coping processes across contexts. Although, the hypothesized relationships among bicultural competence, academic stress and coping processes, adaptive outcomes, and academic resilience (i.e., GPA) were not exactly evident in this analysis as well, Table 7-26 above reveals that there were significant indirect effects of stress, direct action coping, and coping efficacy in the academic context on GPA, and a tendency towards an indirect effect of bicultural competence on GPA via self-esteem. As in the previous model, a direct effect of bicultural competence on GPA was not significant.

An exploratory model was investigated to determine whether an environmental factors (i.e., perceived parental warmth and perceived school discrimination) model provided an alternative explanation of the variables related to academic resilience (i.e., GPA). This model also was tested on the combined ethnic sample for the aforementioned reasons. As in the previous models, the correlation matrix (Table 7-20 above) was referred to in the construction of this model.

On the one hand, Figure 7-4 below reveals that perceived parental warmth was positively and significantly related to both self-esteem (beta = .40) and academic goals (beta = .39). On the other hand, perceived school discrimination was inversely and significantly related to self-esteem (beta = -.32) but not to academic goals. Interestingly, perceived school discrimination was inversely and significantly related directly to GPA (beta = -.24). Lastly, both self-esteem (beta = .13) and academic goals (beta = .21) were positively related to GPA.

Figure 7-4: Environmental Factors Exploratory Model ($\underline{N}$ = 192)

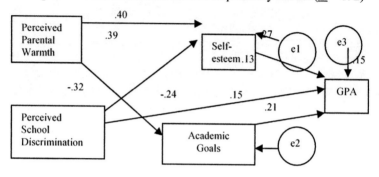

Chi-square = 1.296, $\underline{df}$ = 4, $\underline{p}$ = .862. RMSEA = .000. CFI = 1.000.
RFI = .973.

As shown in Figure 7-4 above, there is an acceptable fit of this model to the data, in that the chi-square value of 1.30 was not statistically significant ($\underline{p}$ = .86). The Root Mean Square Error of Approximation (RMSEA) of .00, the Comparative Fit Index (CFI) of 1.00, and the Relative Fit Index (RFI) of .97, all support the conclusion that this exploratory model also fits the data well. However, Table 7-27 below reveals that only perceived school discrimination was indirectly related to GPA via self-esteem. Perceived parental warmth was not indirectly or directly related to GPA.

Table 7-27. Combined Ethnic Sample (N = 192) Standardized
Indirect/Direct/Total Effects of Environmental Variables on GPA

Variable	Indirect	Direct	Total
Perceived Parental Warmth	.14	. . .	.14
Perceived School Discrimination	.04*	.24	.28
Self-esteem	. . .	.14	.14
Academic Goals	. . .	.21	.21

*$\underline{p}$ < .05.

A total of five structural equation models were explored in this study. The original study model, depicted as a composite model in Figure 7-1 above, had to be modified to explain the relationship between bicultural competence and academic resilience (i.e., GPA). Two alternative study models were developed, one for each domain (i.e., familial and academic). In addition, an exploratory model was investigated to determine whether this model provided an alternative explanation of the factors related to academic resilience (i.e., GPA).

Regarding the tests of the alternative study models, there were marginal indirect relationships between bicultural competence and GPA via self-esteem. Also, there were indirect effects of stress and coping efficacy in the familial context and stress, direct action coping, and coping efficacy in the academic context on GPA via self-esteem. Comparisons between the various fit indices of the two alternative study models revealed that both models similarly fit the data well.

Some interesting observations can be gleaned from the tests of these models. For one, stress (familial) only had a marginal relationship with bicultural competence, but it was independently associated with coping efficacy in the familial context and direct action coping, coping efficacy, and self-esteem in the academic context. Second, bicultural competence was related to social support coping and coping efficacy in the familial context in the expected directions, but to only direct action coping in the academic context. Third, as expected, coping was related to coping efficacy but only in the academic context, not in the familial context. Further, coping efficacy across contexts was directly related to self-esteem and indirectly related to GPA in the expected directions.

It appears that the relationships amongst the stress and coping processes variables differ across contexts. Earlier it was pointed out that there was insufficient evidence to substantiate the premise that stress and coping processes vary as a function of context. However, these findings provide important disconfirming evidence for the coping styles view that posits that individuals cope consistently, regardless of situational demands (see Chapter 4).

The exploratory model sought to understand whether this model provided an alternative explanation of the factors related to academic resilience (i.e., GPA). Although the fit indices revealed a good fit of this model to the data as well, perceived parental warmth was not directly or indirectly related to GPA, whereas perceived school discrimination was only indirectly related to GPA via self-esteem. However, this relationship was significant, whereas the relationships between bicultural competence and academic resilience (i.e., GPA) in the alternative study models were not significant (i.e., marginal relationships). The models explain different phenomena though. Bicultural competence was marginally and indirectly related to academic resilience in the alternative study models, whereas perceived school discrimination was significantly and indirectly related to lower academic resilience or academic vulnerability.

CHAPTER 8

Toward a Model of Drop-Out Prevention

Latina/o youth are widely perceived to be academically at-risk. As stated in Chapter 2, they experience high dropout rates, and there are many studies detailing the types of barriers and obstacles they face (e.g., discrimination and poverty). However, as previously argued, this information does not help us understand individual differences or why it is that some youth thrive despite adversity. Further, a point was made to approach this situation from a strengths as opposed to a deficit perspective. By understanding what factors promote resilience, it was argued that we may not only come to understand individual differences in academic trajectories, but we may also utilize this knowledge to intervene and prevent academic failure in Latina/o youth.

Further, it was pointed out throughout the chapters that not enough studies have looked at academic resilience and the factors that promote the development of this phenomenon in Latina/o youth. This study was an attempt to understand the positive factors that help Latina/o youth to thrive academically despite an at-risk status. Specifically, this study focused on the role of bicultural competence and the mediating variables of stress and coping processes across contexts in academic resilience (i.e., GPA). A model and alternative study models were discussed herein to explain these relationships. The study also included an exploration of the role of the adaptive processes of self-esteem and low depressed mood, academic goals, and the environmental factors of perceived parental warmth and school discrimination in academic resilience (i.e., GPA) to determine whether these models offered better explanations of the study findings.

However, rather than focusing solely on one group, a comparison of Latina/o to Southeast Asian youth was conducted for the following reason. As previously argued cross-cultural studies are effective for disentangling cultural from behavioral variables of a given phenomenon. By conducting a cross-cultural study, we may be better able to determine whether a particular outcome is due to individual or group level factors. It is true that we may gain a level of understanding by conducting an in-depth exploration of the dropout phenomenon in a given group. For example, we may arrive at an understanding of the individual factors that contribute to the phenomenon, such as poverty and a lack of motivation to succeed academically, but we may not come away with an understanding of how culture factors may also leave their imprint. By comparing multiple groups we may be more likely to determine whether an outcome is unique to a particular group, which may indicate that perhaps there is something about the value system of the culture beyond individual factors that also may contribute to the phenomenon. Then again we may determine that the phenomenon is not unique to a particular group, but that multiple groups also share a similar outcome, suggesting that there may be broader societal factors, such as minority status and discrimination that may be contributing to the phenomenon. Asian Americans in general are commonly perceived as a "model minority"; however, the literature suggests that Southeast Asians also may be at-risk academically. Perhaps the groups may reveal interesting differences, or for that matter, similarities in their academic trajectories as a function of sociocultural phenomena (e.g., cultural values or SES).

The primary goals of this study were to provide a link between the acculturation and the stress and coping literatures, and to examine the connections amongst bicultural competence, stress and coping processes across contexts, and academic resilience in a cross-cultural sample (Latina/o and Southeast Asian). The between-group comparisons investigated differences between Latina/o and Southeast Asian groups in bicultural competence, stress and coping processes across contexts, self-esteem, depressed mood, academic goals, perceived parental warmth, perceived school discrimination, and GPA. Group differences in demographics were incorporated into the aforementioned comparisons wherever relevant.

The within-group comparisons examined associations amongst indices of bicultural competence, stress and coping processes across contexts, adaptive processes, environmental factors, and academic variables. Further, a number of structural equation analyses exploring indirect and direct paths were conducted in an effort to understand how sociocultural, psychological, and academic variables may combine to impact academic resilience. Finally, comparisons amongst these models were conducted to pinpoint which model provided the strongest explanation of the relationship between bicultural competence and academic resilience, and to determine the model with the strongest relationship to academic resilience.

In this chapter, outcomes and implications of each of the between-group comparisons (testing the primary hypotheses) will be discussed first, followed by an examination of the highlights of the within-group analyses and the test of the models (testing the secondary hypotheses). Next, general limitations of the study will be explored and directions for future research will be proposed.

The hypothesis that there would be no difference between Latina/o and Southeast Asian youth in bicultural competence was conditionally supported. The Latina/o group initially revealed slightly greater bicultural competence in language as measured with the CBCS than the Southeast Asian group, which is a rather interesting and contradictory finding to the prevailing theory. In Chapter 7, the groups were found to differ significantly in terms of generational status with the Southeast Asian group revealing an immigrant status and the Latina/o group revealing greater generational status in general. As mentioned in Chapter 3, biculturalism, a related construct to bicultural competence, was found to be greater in immigrant families and in first and second-generation children of immigrants (Buriel, 1993). Also, research has found that immigrant groups reveal greater achievement press and greater motivation to become bicultural out of sheer necessity than more established groups (see Gonzalez & Padilla, 1997; Rumbaut, 2000; Suárez-Orozco & Suárez-Orozco, 2001). Therefore, according to the literature the Southeast Asian group would be expected to reveal greater bicultural competence, which was not the case in this study.

Even though the literature portrays immigrants as revealing greater motivation to become bicultural than more established groups, apparently Southeast Asian youth in this study were not as motivated as the Latina/o group were to maintain dual language competency. Latina/o youth despite their greater generational status were managing to preserve competencies in both their ethnic language and in the English language according to personal reports. As aforementioned, ethnic language competency has been found to decrease significantly with greater generational status. This is a rather interesting finding, which suggests that bicultural competence in language may be viewed as a greater resilience factor for some youth, therefore it is fostered. As mentioned in Chapter 3, bicultural competence is argued to be a significant protective factor for acculturating groups. Latina/o youth may view greater benefits for biculturalism than the Southeast Asian adolescents do. Perhaps dual language maintenance affords such youth with a sense of commonality, serving as an affirmation of their shared ethnic identification. Also likely is the possibility that the Southeast Asian group has not had sufficient time to develop biculturalism as the more established Latina/o group. Given more time, perhaps the groups would be more similar in terms of dual language maintenance.

It is interesting that the groups only differed in bicultural competence in language, and not in identity and values. Identity and values may not change as quickly as language, especially when there is the impetus to acculturate. Theoretically, this phenomenon is supported. As mentioned in Chapter 3, the related constructs of bicultural identity and bicultural self-identification are believed to be later emerging phenomena, typically consolidated in adulthood (see Phinney, 1993). Bicultural competence, which is a broader construct including language, identity, and values, appears to be an earlier developing phenomenon. Therefore, one would expect to see changes in bicultural competence in language before changes in identity and values become evident.

However, since the groups were found to differ significantly in terms of generational status, this factor was controlled for in the analysis. Indeed, after controlling for generational status, a greater group difference was found for the bicultural competence language dimension still in favor of the Latina/o group, further discounting the theory of greater bicultural competence in immigrant populations. According to the theory there would be no difference between the groups in bicultural competence when controlling for generational status, which was not the case herein. This finding is significant in that it provides contradictory evidence against the prevalent notion of biculturalism being greater in immigrant groups.

In Chapter 7, the groups were found to differ markedly on socioeconomic status (SES), with the Latina/o group reporting a much higher SES level than the Southeast Asian respondents did; therefore, it was deemed necessary to control for this factor in the analysis. Interestingly, when controlling for parental SES, the group difference in bicultural competence in language disappeared. It appears that bicultural competence may be more sensitive to SES than generational status. This finding adds credence to LaFromboise, Coleman, and Gerton's (1993) assertion, previously mentioned in Chapter 3, that socioeconomic status may be a significant factor influencing an individual's ability to develop and refine the necessary skills for bicultural competence. Unfortunately, these researchers did not elaborate on why this may be so. Perhaps a higher SES may influence a greater degree of development of bicultural competence because of increased opportunities and resources (e.g., greater access to computers or to tutorial services).

Nevertheless, as previously mentioned, parents of Gandara's (1995) biculturally competent and academically resilient sample created an "achievement press" in their home for higher academic performance, despite the lack of economic resources, by providing their children with access to ideas, information, and technologies, for example. Families with a higher SES may have more access to these and other types of resources that also foster cultural competence, creating an "achievement press" for bicultural competence, which may be the case for the Latina/o families of the study. However, the Southeast Asian group revealed a greater "achievement press" for academic resilience as indicated by both their higher GPA and academic goals overall as compared to the Latina/o group (see Chapter7). Southeast Asian families were successful at creating an "achievement press" for academic resilience despite the lack of economic resources. Studies confirm that Asian Americans in general reveal greater academic achievement press than other ethnic groups (see Fuligni, 1997; Rumbaut, 2000). Results from the Children of Immigrants Longitudinal Study (CILS) suggests that high academic expectations and educational ambitiousness in both parents and children is related to greater academic achievement in Asian youth (Rumbaut, 2000). In sum, with equable SES, no differences between Latina/o and Southeast Asian subjects in bicultural competence in language were evident.

It was thought that the groups also would not differ on stress and coping processes across contexts. Contrary to these hypotheses, differences were found on these items and indices for the groups of study. Interestingly, significant group differences were found only in the familial stressful situation. First, the Latina/o group was more likely to report major problems in the familial context than the

Southeast Asian group. Second, the Latina/o group also reported greater stress in the familial situation in contrast to the Southeast Asian group. The groups did not differ in coping processes across contexts or in academic stress/ors, however.

Overall, then, this pattern suggests that the Latina/o subjects were more likely to report both major stressors and more stress in the familial situation than the Southeast Asian subjects did. Adolescence is commonly viewed as a time when major changes occur in family, school, and peer group structures (see Petersen & Hamburg, 1986). Not surprisingly, studies have found that the most commonly reported problems amongst adolescents are social, relating to family and peers (see Stark, Spirito, Williams, & Guevremont, 1989; Wagner & compas, 1990). Thus, familial stressors appear to be normative for adolescents. Nevertheless, they appear to be more salient for the Latina/o group.

Interestingly, the literature suggests that the Southeast Asian group should reveal greater stress than the Latina/o group. According to the studies reviewed in Chapter 4, immigrant populations are believed to be exposed to another level of stressors on top of the normative stressors youth encounter, which include different cultural values, English proficiency problems, minority status, exposure to racial/ethnic stereotypes, prejudice, discrimination, and reduction in available social supports (see Sue, Sue, Sue, & Takeuchi, 1995). Based on these assumptions, one would expect that the Southeast Asian group would reveal greater stress/ors, which was not the case.

A possible explanation for this disparity may be ascertained from respondent's household characteristics. In Chapter 7, it was revealed that the Latina/o group's parents were more likely to be divorced or separated. In fact, the percentage of Latinas/os reporting separation or divorce was almost five times greater than that of the Southeast Asian group (see Table 7-5). However, Chapter 7 also revealed that the Southeast Asian group was more impoverished (also see Table 7-5). Apparently, this condition did not contribute to greater rates of familial stress/ors for this group. On the other hand, marital instability may have negatively impacted the Latina/o group as they reported greater stress/ors in the familial context. It may be that marital instability may be a more significant stressor than poverty for the groups.

Research appears to support this conclusion. Ge et al. (1992) found that familial economic pressure did not exert a direct effect on adolescent adjustment, but rather it exerted an indirect effect via its effects on marital quality. In other words, familial economic pressure inversely affected marital quality, which in turn was associated with adolescent emotional distress. Familial economic pressure did not directly affect adolescent adjustment; this path was not significant. This finding supports the conclusion that marital instability may be more damaging for adolescent adjustment than an environmental factor such as poverty.

Rumbaut (2000) points out that family structure is a "key determinant of educational performance outcomes--as well as of self-esteem and depression." According to this researcher, the presence of an intact family structure for youth may be associated with academic resilience. Based on the recent results of the Children of Immigrants Longitudinal Study (CILS), the largest study of its kind to systematically explore the relationship between educational performance and psychological adaptation, youth who reported greater family stability, both structurally and emotionally, revealed greater educational achievement and academic aspirations, higher self-esteem, and lower depressive symptoms (Rumbaut, 2000).

In sum, the Latinas/os were reporting significantly greater familial marital dysfunction as compared to the Southeast Asian group, which may account for their greater rate of familial stress/ors, and their lower academic goals and GPA. Acculturation appears to come at a price, which is especially true for the Latina/o group. The Latinas/os rate of separation and divorce more closely resembles that of the general U.S. rate (i.e., approximately 50%) (see Table 7-5). It appears that the Southeast Asian's immigrant status may be more protective for marital stability.

Interestingly, although the Southeast Asian group reported lower levels of SES, they did not report greater stress in the familial or the academic contexts than the Latina/o group. In Chapter 2, it was discussed that low SES is a significant risk factor for poor academic performance for ethnic youth (see National Research Council, 1993). Consequently, one would expect that this group would report greater stress in the academic context than the Latina/o group; however, this was not the case. Interestingly, in Chapter 4, Latina/o students were noted to experience academic stressors as more stressful than Anglo students (see Vazquez & Garcia-Vazquez, 1995). However, there were no differences in academic stress/ors between the Latina/o and

Southeast Asian groups. These findings are noteworthy in that they provide disconfirming evidence for these assumptions, and they underscore the possibility that there may be other factors present in the lives of these youths, which mediate outcomes to promote resilience.

However, it is also possible that the stress questions may have been experienced differently for the groups. A common dilemma discussed extensively in cross-cultural methodology is that the same questions may have diverse cultural meanings for different ethnic groups. Thus, the Latina/o and Southeast Asian respondents may not actually be responding to the same questions. Perhaps, the groups interpreted the familial stress/ors questions vastly different. For the Latina/o group, these questions may have been interpreted more negatively, whereas for the Southeast Asian group, these same questions may have been more innocuous.

Gender differences were found only for social support coping in the familial context. Latina and Southeast Asian females revealed greater familial social support coping than Latino and Southeast Asian males. This finding is consistent with the empirical evidence discussed in Chapter 4 that females report greater use of social support coping than males. Stark, Spirito, Williams, and Guevremont (1989) found that adolescent females reported greater use of social support coping than adolescent males in their sample of 14 to 17 year-old, primarily White high school students. Girls were found to use this strategy more with problems encountered with friends. However, Compas, Malcarne, and Fondacaro (1988) found that adolescent females reported greater use of emotion-focused coping with academic situations than adolescent males. Studies on adults have found more frequent use of both emotion-focused and social support coping strategies for females (see Billings & Moos, 1981; Stone & Neale, 1984). In this study, gender differences were found only for social support coping and solely in the familial context, which is consistent with Stark et al.'s finding, despite the differences in the ethnic composition of the samples.

Stress and coping processes also were compared cross-situationally with some rather interesting results. Rather than finding that coping differs as a function of context, support for the central premise of the coping styles view that individuals cope consistently, regardless of situational demands, was found. No differences in stress ratings, direct action coping, social support coping, and coping efficacy were found across contexts (i.e., familial and academic) (see Table 7-10).

However, differences were found for stressors and stress appraisals across contexts (see Table 7-8 and 7-12). Not surprisingly, minor problems were more likely to be reported in the academic situation, whereas major problems were more likely to be reported in the familial context. Further, both Latina/o and Southeast Asian youth were more likely to appraise the academic problem as a challenge than the familial problem.

The alternative study models discussed below provided further evidence against this view, and support the coping processes theory discussed in Chapter 4, which stipulates that individuals alter their coping behavior flexibly and adaptively, depending upon the situation. Comparisons of the two alternative study models reveal that the relationships amongst the bicultural competence, stress and coping processes, and outcome variables differed across contexts. In sum, the findings appear to substantiate to some extent that stress and coping processes vary as a function of context.

It was expected that the groups would not differ in self-esteem, which was the case. It is interesting that despite the Southeast Asian group's lower SES, no differences in self-esteem were evident. Moreover, despite the Latina/o group's greater rate of parental divorce or separation, coupled with their greater familial stress/or, these factors did not contribute to lower self-esteem. This pattern also suggests that other factors may be mediating outcomes for the groups.

Similarly, it was expected that the groups would not differ in depressed mood, which also was the case. No differences in depressed mood were detected despite the impact of these significant stressors for the groups. This finding is noteworthy given that familial stress was significantly associated with depressed mood in Table 7-19. Consequently, the Latina/o group was expected to report greater depressed mood than the Southeast Asian group, which was not the case though. Again, this suggests that there may be other factors mediating the relationship between these environmental and outcome factors for the youth.

What factors could possibly promote resilience for these youths? In Chapter 2, the concept of protective factors or "buffers" was introduced. Protective factors, such as personal resources (e.g., temperament) and environmental resources (e.g., high SES), are believed to reduce the likelihood of dysfunction in the presence of vulnerabilities and stressful life experiences. In Chapter 3, it was argued that bicultural competence might be a significant personal protective factor for Latina/o and Southeast Asian youth. Quite possibly, bicultural competence may be a source of resilience for these youths, buffering the impact of environmental stressors (i.e., familial marital instability and poverty).

Although it was expected that there would be no group differences in GPA and academic goals, significant differences were found herein for the groups. The Southeast Asian group outperformed the Latina/o group on GPA and revealed greater academic goals. Immigrant groups were noted to outdo more established groups on academic performance (see Chapter 2). It was noted in Chapter 3 that immigrant parents are believed to pass on their high aspirations to their children. Further, academic performance also was noted in Chapter 3 to decrease with greater generational status for some ethnic youth.

Nevertheless, this finding is particularly noteworthy given that low SES has been found to be associated repeatedly and consistently with poor academic performance, as discussed in Chapter 2 (see National Research Council, 1993). As previously pointed out, research has shown that impoverished youth are more likely than their more advantaged peers to do poorly in school and to be vulnerable to school failure (see Children's Defense Fund, 1991; Perez & Duany, 1992). Despite this risk factor, Southeast Asians were able to outperform Latinas/os academically. What possible explanation could there be to account for the difference in academic outcomes between Latina/o and Southeast Asian youth?

It is possible that Latinas/os greater familial stressful environments may selectively and negatively impact GPA but not adjustment; however, GPA was not found to correlate significantly with familial stress (see Table 7-19). The acculturation literature may provide us with some insight into this phenomenon. In Chapter 3, Ogbu (1978) and Gibson and Ogbu (1991) argued that later generation ethnic students are more sensitive to ongoing patterns of discrimination and prejudice than immigrant students, which in turn may culminate in alienation from school and giving up on education. It appears that prolonged exposure to racism and discrimination may sensitize youth, eroding their "achievement press", which may be especially true for the more established Latina/o ethnic group. However, both groups reported equal rates of perceived school discrimination. Nevertheless, perceptions and feelings are distinct phenomena. Although the groups are reporting equal rates of perceptions of school discrimination, it is possible that the Latina/o group may be sensitive to school discrimination than the Southeast Asian group.

Gender differences also were found for GPA. Latina and Southeast Asian females revealed higher GPAs than Latino and Southeast Asian males. This finding is consistent with the empirical evidence, which finds that females consistently outperform males academically as discussed in Chapter 2. For example, in Gonzalez and Padilla's (1997) aforementioned study of 2,169 Mexican American students from three California high schools, academically resilient students were more likely to be female. Gandara (1995) also noted significant gender differences in her sample. As previously mentioned, most female high-achievers in Gandara's study were consistently good students who tended to aspire to college early in their school careers, whereas the male high-achievers revealed a more uneven picture of academic development.

As hypothesized, no group differences were found on perceptions of parental warmth and school discrimination. Interestingly, both groups equally perceived their parent(s) as caring and supportive even though the Latinas/os reported greater familial stress/ors and higher rates of parental divorce or separation. Apparently, these families still managed to be caring and supportive to the youth despite the inherent stressfulness of their familial situations. Perhaps the Latina/o group's greater economic resources or their greater bicultural competence helped the youth and their families to offset the potentially damaging effects of familial stress on well-being.

It is not surprising that both groups perceived equal rates of school discrimination since individuals with minority status have been noted to be exposed to racism and discrimination as discussed in Chapter 2. However, as aforementioned, the Latina/o group may be more sensitive to school discrimination than the Southeast Asian group because of their greater generational status and consequently, their greater exposure to discrimination, despite the sample's reports of equal rates of perceived school discrimination.

WITHIN-GROUP PATTERNS

The hypothesized relationships among the bicultural competence, stress and coping processes across contexts, exploratory adaptive variables, and academic resilience (i.e., GPA) were presented in a composite model in Figure 7-1. However, this model was found to be ineffective at explaining the relationships amongst these variables, hence alternative study models were developed. Figures 7-2 and 7-3 presented these alternative study models, which utilized the correlation matrix (Table 7-19). Figure 7-4 presented the results of an exploratory analysis, investigating the relationships among environmental factors, adaptive processes, and academic variables, which also utilized the correlation matrix (Table 7-20). In this section, key patterns from the correlation analyses and findings for selected components of the structural equation models will be integrated and discussed.

Although the hypothesized relationships amongst the variables of interest were not entirely substantiated, some rather interesting associations were evident. It is noteworthy that in both alternative study models, which investigated the relationships among bicultural competence, stress and coping processes across contexts, adaptive processes, and academic resilience (i.e., GPA), bicultural competence was not related to stress as hypothesized, but it was related to coping processes and self-esteem (see below). However, inspection of the correlation matrix (Table 7-19) reveals that bicultural competence in values and identity was significantly associated only with familial stress, not academic stress.

Unexpectedly, the findings indicate that bicultural competence in values and identity may be related to greater not lower familial stress as hypothesized. Evidently, the process of becoming biculturally competent may be fraught with stress for ethnic youth and their families. Perhaps the youth may be acculturating more quickly than their parents, which may cause conflict between the adolescents and their parents. Classic acculturation theory appears to support this perspective. From this perspective, the process of acculturation and biculturalism is viewed as a stressful experience both economically and psychologically because it reinforces second-class citizenship and alienation of the individual acclimating to a new culture (see Chapter 3). The individual experiencing this process may forge a unique identity, a bicultural identity, which may be an all-together different identity formation than that of one's parents. Consequently, bicultural youth may feel different from their parents, and may experience a sense of alienation from one's family.

Equally likely is the possibility that a stressful familial context may spur some youth on to developing competencies and resources elsewhere. As previously discussed, bicultural competence may be a significant personal source of resilience for at-risk youth. The theory discussed in Chapter 3 and the study findings appear to suggest this. Perhaps, a stressful familial situation may spur some youth to become biculturally competent which, in turn, may reward their competencies through, for example, increased attention and acknowledgment from one's teachers, friends, or family. It is interesting that bicultural competence was not associated with academic stress. Perhaps the academic context is not experienced as stressful as the familial context for biculturally competent individuals because of greater exposure to others who may be similarly developing bicultural competence.

Further, the findings indicate that bicultural competence may be related to the coping processes of social support coping, direct action coping, coping efficacy, and to self-esteem. This finding is significant because no studies have been found that have linked bicultural competence to coping processes. Some studies suggest that there may be relationships amongst the phenomena; but no study has attempted to determine these relationships systematically. However, these relationships receive sample theoretical support as discussed in Chapters 3 and 4 (also see Berry, 1998; LaFromboise, Coleman, & Gerton, 1993). The findings provide important empirical evidence linking bicultural competence to greater social support coping in the familial context and to greater direct action coping in the academic context. Bicultural competence also was significantly associated with greater coping efficacy and self-esteem.

The importance of these findings is further underscored because this process was found to be highly adaptive. For one, bicultural competence and coping efficacy across contexts were associated with greater self-esteem. Second, greater self-esteem in turn was found to be related to higher GPA. Third, there were marginal (i.e., not statistically significant) indirect relationships of bicultural competence to GPA via coping efficacy across contexts and self-esteem. Bicultural competence appears to be somewhat related to resilience. Specifically, it appears to be related to greater coping efficacy across contexts and to self-esteem, which in turn may be somewhat related to higher GPA.

In sum, the findings provide empirical evidence to partially substantiate the theory of the mediating role of stress and coping processes across contexts, and adaptive processes in the relationship between bicultural competence and academic resilience (i.e., GPA). The findings also provide some support for the resources model of coping, which stipulates that personal and social resources are related to subsequent mental health both directly and indirectly, through adaptive coping responses as discussed in Chapter 4 (Holahan, Valentiner, & Moos, 1995). A direct route from bicultural competence to academic resilience (i.e., GPA) was not evident. However, the findings provide partial support for a mediating or indirect relationship between bicultural competence and academic resilience (i.e., GPA). Further, the models provide important evidence linking acculturation to stress and coping processes across contexts, adaptive processes, and academic outcomes. Lastly, the alternative study models revealed slightly different relationships amongst the stress and coping processes variables as a function of context, substantiating the hypothesis that stress and coping processes vary as a function of context, as previously discussed.

This exploratory model sought to determine whether the environmental factors of perceived parental warmth and perceived school discrimination were more strongly related to academic resilience (i.e., GPA) than the personal resource of bicultural competence. This model revealed that perceived parental warmth was related to greater self-esteem and higher academic goals, which in turn were related to higher GPA. However, this analysis revealed that perceived parental warmth was not significantly, directly or indirectly, associated with GPA via self-esteem and academic goals (see Table 7-27). This finding is noteworthy because in contradicts the prevalent theory and ample empirical evidence discussed in Chapter 2 that a significant factor in Latina/o academic performance is parental support.

On the other hand, perceived school discrimination was related to self-esteem and GPA. This analysis revealed that perceived school discrimination was significantly and indirectly associated with GPA via self-esteem. Greater perceptions of school discrimination were associated with lower self-esteem, which in turn was associated with lower GPA. However, this model cannot be compared to the alternative models to determine which model is more effective at explaining academic resilience (i.e., GPA) since this model is not a resilience model per se, but rather it appears to be an academic vulnerability model.

It is interesting that perceived parental warmth was not related to GPA, whereas perceived school discrimination was related to GPA. Perceptions of school discrimination appear to impact GPA greater than perceptions of parental warmth. This model is noteworthy in that it substantiates the ecological theory of the importance of environmental factors for adolescent behavior and development, as discussed in Chapter 5. The theory and empirical evidence discussed in Chapter 2 appears to support the assertion that school discrimination may be highly stressful for ethnic youth, which ultimately may discourage their continued attendance, motivation, and performance.

In addition to the limitations discussed above, several other caveats pertaining to the design, internal and external validity, analyses, and measurement should be mentioned. A major potential threat to the internal validity of the study was reporting biases of the adolescent participants. On the stress and coping processes across contexts items and measure, youths were asked to recall a recent stressful event in the familial and academic contexts. Because of their youth, the participants of the study may not have been able to recall a specific stressful event in enough detail to provide accurate information about the situation, and how they coped with the problem.

Further, six youths were unable to recall a recent stressful event and needed assistance. Unknowingly, the research assistants could have influenced subjects' responses on this measure. Interestingly, some subjects, despite the research assistants' efforts, still did not have a stressful event to report on. It is plausible that some youth do not experience significant stressors in their lives or perceive significant stressors as innocuous. Also likely is the possibility that some youth do not feel comfortable in disclosing their problems to individuals unfamiliar to them. Then again, some youth may be in denial of their problems.

Another significant limitation of the study was the cross-sectional study design and the lack of a longitudinal design. Since this study was a dissertation study, a longitudinal design was considered impractical; a cross-sectional study design was deemed more appropriate. However, a cross-sectional study design merely captures a snapshot of the phenomena of interest, and certainly cannot account for causality or change as can a longitudinal study design. This study could have been expanded into a longitudinal study with more time and resources. A longitudinal design may be instrumental for tracking developmental changes in bicultural competence, and its relationship with other variables over time.

Neither of the subsamples in this study can be considered representative. Both groups were self-selected, and met the ethnic and grade criteria. Further, because of the study's requirements (i.e., sitting at a desk in a classroom setting while filling out a questionnaire for 30-45 minutes), individuals who were unmotivated, and especially at-risk academically, may have been unwilling to participate. To counteract motivational constraints, subjects were reimbursed for their participation with $5.00. Nevertheless, the sample may still be over-represented by relatively high-functioning, biculturally competent respondents. Therefore, the findings of the study probably would not apply to individuals who are not biculturally competent or to monocultural populations.

Further, the findings may not generalize to other academically and socioeconomically at-risk ethnic groups, such as Native Americans and African Americans, which is another constraint of the study. Because of time and economic constraints, it was not possible to include more ethnic groups in this cross-cultural study. Therefore, the findings may only generalize to Latinas/os and Southeast Asians with similar sociocultural demographics. Another limitation of the analyses was the smaller size of the Southeast Asian group (n = 89) relative to the Latina/o group (n = 103), which prevented the possibility of conducting separate structural equation analyses for the groups.

Also, had the study utilized a longitudinal design, it may have been possible to conduct path analyses to increase our understanding of the factors that predict academic resilience. Since the study did not utilize a longitudinal design, a precise understanding of cause and effect was sacrificed for practicality. As previously discussed, the use of self-report measures was a primary limitation of the present study. Although our research assistants were trained to detect suspicious responses (e.g., answering all questions on a given page with the same numbered response) and to watch for respondents filling out their questionnaires much too quickly or slowly, it was not possible to prevent all people from responding inaccurately or dishonestly to the self-report measures. Some self-report measures utilize questions specifically designed to detect inaccurate or dishonest responses, however. The measures utilized herein may be improved in the future with the addition of these types of questions.

Another significant limitation of the study was the measure of coping strategies utilized herein. As aforementioned, this measure utilized only one item to assess each coping strategy and thus, could not account for enough variability. This limitation may explain why the coping variables did not correlate as expected with the other variables of interest. An optimal coping measure would utilize four to six different items to assess each coping strategy. The use of GPA as a proxy indicator of academic resilience was another limitation of the study. Although GPA may be an indicator of an aspect of academic resilience (i.e., performance), it may not completely capture this phenomenon. A specific measure of academic resilience would have been ideal, although a comprehensive search failed to find a specific measure of academic resilience. Most studies reviewed herein utilized standardized test scores and/or GPA as indicators of academic resilience.

A further limitation of the study may be experimenter bias. All questionnaires were administered by this investigator and her assistants, who were aware of the study's hypotheses; thereby increasing the potential for experimenter bias, for example, by unconsciously influencing subjects' responses to support the study's hypotheses. Lastly, another study limitation was the reliance on only subjects' reports of parental warmth and school discrimination. A superior design would include the responses of multiple informants on these measures, such as parents, other siblings, teachers, and counselors, to corroborate the findings. However, because of the nature of the study (i.e., dissertation) and the funding limitations, these options were outside the scope of the study.

An explanation for the apparent lack of studies finding a relationship between bicultural competence and academic resilience may be because they have failed to investigate the role of mediating variables in this relationship. Future examinations of the relationship between bicultural competence and academic resilience should, first and foremost, investigate the role of various mediating variables in this relationship. The current study suggested that coping processes might mediate the relationship between bicultural competence and academic resilience. Further investigation of the mediating role of coping processes in this relationship might be interesting. For example, researchers could examine how different coping strategies, such as emotion-focused coping, adaptive processes, and academic variables mediate the relationship between bicultural competence and academic resilience. This type of study might utilize a different measure of coping strategies because of the aforementioned constraints.

Also, it would be interesting to conduct further studies on the relationship between environmental factors, adaptive processes, and academic outcomes. The study suggests that perceptions of school discrimination may be related to lower GPA via lower self-esteem. Perceived parental warmth was neither directly nor indirectly related to GPA, however. It would be interesting to validate these research findings further and to conduct more studies on these relationships. Future examinations might explore the role of other mediating variables in these relationships. For example, self-esteem may not mediate the relationship between perceptions of parental warmth and academic resilience; however, there may be other variables, which were not explored herein, that do mediate this relationship.

Further, longitudinal examinations of bicultural competence and academic resilience appear merited. From Chapter 3, it was understood that there is a developmental progression inherent in biculturalism. For example, bilingualism appears to develop earlier than a bicultural identity formation. An explanation for the lack of significance in the relationship between bicultural competence and academic resilience (i.e., GPA) may be because the youth may not have sufficiently developed competence in the two cultures by the 9th-grade. Perhaps the relationship between bicultural competence and academic resilience may strengthen over time. Future studies might benefit from utilizing older adolescents to study these relationships and/or by conducting regularly scheduled follow-ups on subjects.

Comparative cross-cultural studies also are warranted. For example, these relationships may be explored with different cultural or ethnic groups in the U.S. or abroad to determine whether there are differences in these relationships as a function of ethnicity. The study should be replicated with socioculturally similar and dissimilar groups to substantiate the findings.

In sum, future examinations of the relationships between bicultural competence and academic resilience, and environmental factors and academic resilience should be conducted with larger samples. Attempts should be made to utilize a longitudinal design to understand causality and change, and to include more ethnic groups in such studies. A longitudinal design and bigger samples would provide the statistical power necessary to test separate path models, examining the different predictors of academic resilience across multiple ethnic groups.

Despite its limitations, the study suggests some areas that could be the focus of intervention and prevention efforts. For academically at-risk ethnic youth, such as Latinas/os, programs designed to promote bicultural competence might be effective for enhancing effective coping, increasing coping efficacy, self-esteem, and GPA, thereby promoting academic success, and reducing or preventing early school exit.

Because of the complexity of the relationships amongst the variables investigated herein, such a dropout prevention program must be multi-faceted. It is suggested that for a successful dropout prevention and intervention program for academically at-risk ethnic youth, the following central components should be included: (a) bicultural competence skill development, utilizing LaFromboise et al.'s (1993) aforementioned criteria, (b) self-esteem enhancement, (c) promotion of effective coping strategies across contexts, and (d) effective management skills to combat school discrimination. Research projects should be undertaken to evaluate the effectiveness of the program. For a truly effective program, ideally, partnerships between researchers, students, parents, and schools should be undertaken to enhance the goals of the program and to develop strategies to counter structural inequality (i.e., racism).

This study was one of few of its kind to provide a link among the acculturation, stress and coping processes across contexts, adaptive processes, and academic literatures by examining both (1) the relationship between bicultural competence and academic resilience (i.e., GPA), and (2) the role of the mediating variables of stress and coping processes across contexts and adaptive processes in this relationship, in a cross-cultural sample. This study was the first systematic investigation of the associations among bicultural competence, stress and coping processes across contexts, self-esteem, and academic resilience in Latina/o and Southeast Asian youth. The findings are significant, because they provide crucial empirical evidence substantiating the theory of the positive benefits of bicultural competence.

This study also provided an important link between the ecological literature and the academic literature by examining both (1) the relationships amongst perceived school discrimination, perceived parental warmth, and academic resilience (i.e., GPA), and (2) the role of the mediating variable of self-esteem and academic goals in this relationship, in a cross-cultural sample. This finding also is significant because it provides crucial empirical evidence substantiating the theory of the negative ramifications of school discrimination on well-being and academic outcomes.

In sum, an understanding of the connections amongst these factors may have important implications for designing dropout prevention and intervention programs for educationally at-risk ethnic youth. The findings suggest that dropout prevention and intervention programs should promote bicultural competence, self-esteem, effective coping with school discrimination and across divers situations, which ultimately may boost resilience.

Appendix A: Subject Questioonnaire

BACKGROUND INFORMATION

This questionnaire is anonymous; no one else besides this researcher, a research assistant, and the researchers' supervisor will see this questionnaire. Your name on this questionnaire is not necessary; <u>you will not</u> be identified by your name in this study. We are interested in some general information about yourself. There are no right or wrong answers. Please think carefully about each question before you answer it. If you find a question where none of the answer choices are true, please circle the "other" category and write in your answer on the line next to it. Also, when you see a question with a blank next to it, please fill-in the blank with the appropriate response. Thank you.

1. *What is your sex? (Circle one)*   1. female   2. male

2. *What is your age?* _____

3. *In what country(ies) were your family members born? If you don't know, say so in the blank.*
you: _____   mother: _____
father: _____   grandparents: _____
great-grandparents: _____

4. *What is your ethnic identity?* _____

5. *What languages do you speak?* _____

6. *Do you currently work for pay? (Circle one)*   1. Yes   2. No
If you answered yes, how many hours per week do you currently work? _____

7. *Are your parents separated or divorced? (Circle one)*   1. Yes   2. No

8. *How many family members live with you? Please write in the number of each.*

sisters: _____   brothers: _____   parents: _____   step-siblings: _____
step-parent: ___   cousins: _____   aunts: _____   uncles: _____
grandparents: _____   other: _____

9. *Please put a check in the appropriate spaces. Are you:*
1st born _____,   *2nd born* _____,   *3rd born* _____,   *4th born* _____,
5th born _____,   *6th or more* _____,   *or last born* _____ *in your family?*

10. *What grades do you usually get? (Circle one):*
   1. Mostly As   2. Mostly Bs   3. Mostly Cs   4. Mostly Ds   5. Mostly Fs

11. *The major source(s) of income for your household (people you live with most of the time) is (Circle all that apply):*
   1. Earnings from work
   2. Welfare
   3. Child or spousal support
   4. Social security, Disability, or other govt. benefits
   5. Assistance from family members or friends
   6. Other (please specify): _____

12. *What kind of job does your father have?* _____, *and what kind of job does your mother have?* _____.
   If applicable, what kind of job does your step-mother have? _____;
or what kind of job does your step-father have? _____.

13. *What is the highest grade level completed by the following family members? (enter the corresponding number in the spaces below)*
   (1).   your father: _____   (2).   your mother: _____
         1. 0 = no schooling   2. 1st - 4th grade or equivalent
         3. 5th - 8th grade or equivalent   4. some high school or equivalent
         5. high school graduate or equivalent 6. some college or university ed.
         7. college or university graduate   8. graduate education/degree
         9. post-graduate education   10. unknown

14. *What kind of activities do you and your closest family members regularly (one or more times a year) engage in? (Circle all that apply)*
         1. travel outside of California   2. attend concerts, plays, or symph.
         3. go to restaurants   4. go to a theme park (e.g., Disney)
         5. movies at a theatre   6. visit an art/science museum
         7. take vacations   8. go clothes shopping
         9. we don't do any of these   10. other (specify):_____

ON THE NEXT PAGE, WE WOULD LIKE YOU TO ANSWER SOME QUESTIONS ABOUT YOUR CULTURAL VALUES OR BELIEFS.

Attitudes Survey

We want to know if you strongly agree or disagree with some statements. If you strongly agree, enter a 9 in the blank space; if you strongly disagree, enter a 1 in that space; if you are unsure, enter a 5 next to the statement. In short, use this key:

Strongly Disagree							**Strongly Agree**	
1	2	3	4	5	6	7	8	9

1. I prefer to say what's on my mind when I talk with people_____
2. My happiness depends very much on the happiness of those around me_____
3. I would do what would please my family, even if I didn't like that activity_____
4. One should live one's life independently of others_____
5. It is important for me to maintain harmony within my group (family or friends)_____
6. It is important to me that I do my job or school work better than others_____
7. I enjoy working in situations involving competition with others_____
8. The well-being of my group (family or friends) is important to me_____
9. I enjoy being unique and different from others in many ways_____
10. I often do "my own thing"_____
11. To me, pleasure is spending time with others_____
12. When another person does better than I do, I get annoyed or bothered_____
13. I would sacrifice an activity that I enjoy very much if my family did not approve of it_____
14. Children should be taught to place duty before pleasure_____
15. I hate to disagree with others in my group (family or friends)_____
16. Winning is everything_____

ON THE NEXT TWO PAGES, WE ARE GOING TO ASK YOU ABOUT TYPES OF PROBLEMS YOU DEAL WITH.

Stress and Coping Questionnaire

1. For the following questions, we want to know how you deal with the stress in your life. We would like for you to think about the <u>last stressful event</u> that happened to <u>you personally</u> that was related to a <u>problem at home with a parent, parent figure, or other close family member</u>. Could you please briefly describe that event and when it occurred.

A. description of event:_____

B. date of this event:_____

2. *How stressful was this low point for you? By "stressful" we mean how troubling or disturbing it was to you. Please circle the number which best describes this, where 1 = Little or no stress, and 7 = Most stressful thing ever experienced.*

Little or no stress   **Most stress**

     1   2   3   4   5   6   7

3. *Would you say that this event was primarily (circle all that apply):*

    1. A threat   2. A harm

    3. A loss   4. A challenge

    5. An annoyance   6. A threat/harm to a loved one

    7. Something you felt helpless about

    8. Something you felt ashamed of

    9. Other (explain): _____

4. *People have different ways of dealing with problems. As you look back on the **family related problem** you just described, how often did you do each of the following things?*

	Not at all	Used a little	Used somewhat	Used a lot
1. Did you turn your attention away from the problem by thinking about other things or getting involved in some activity?	0	1	2	3
2. Did you try to see the problem in a different light that made it seem more bearable?	0	1	2	3
3. Did you think about solutions to the problem, and did something to try to solve it?	0	1	2	3
4. Did you express feelings in response to the problem to reduce tension, anxiety, or frustration?	0	1	2	3
5. Did you accept that the problem had occurred, but that nothing could be done?	0	1	2	3

6. Did you seek or find emotional social support from loved ones, friends, or professionals?	0	1	2	3
7. Did you do something with the specific purpose of relaxing?	0	1	2	3
8. Did you seek or find spiritual or religious comfort?	0	1	2	3

5. *How did you feel that you handled this problem overall? (choose one)*
1. Not well at all   2. Not too well   3. OK   4. Fairly well   5.Very well

6. *Now I would like you to repeat the previous questions about stress and coping but this time I would like for you to think about a <u>recent stressful event</u> that happened to <u>you personally</u> that was related to a <u>problem at school involving school staff, classmates, or your school performance.</u> Could you please briefly describe that event and when it occurred.*
A. description of event:_____
B. date of this event:_____

7. *How stressful was this low point for you? By "stressful" we mean how troubling or disturbing it was to you. Please circle the number which best describes this, where 1 = Little or no stress, and 7 = Most stressful thing ever experienced.*

  Little or no stress   **Most stress**
      1   **2**   **3**   **4**   **5**   **6**   **7**

8. *Would you say that this event was primarily (circle all that apply):*
    1. A threat   2. A harm
    3. A loss   4. A challenge
    5. An annoyance   6. A threat/harm to a loved one
    7. Something you felt helpless about
    8. Something you felt ashamed of
    9. Other (explain): _____

9. *People have different ways of dealing with problems. As you look back on the **school related problem** you just described, how often did you do each of the following things?*

	Not at all	Used a little	Used somewhat	Used a lot
1. Did you turn your attention away from the problem by thinking about other things or getting involved in some activity?	0	1	2	3

2. Did you try to see the problem in
a different light that made it seem
more bearable?   0   1   2   3
3. Did you think about solutions to
the problem, and did something to
try to solve it?   0   1   2   3
4. Did you express feelings in
response to the problem to reduce
tension, anxiety, or frustration?   0   1   2   3
5. Did you accept that the problem had occurred, but that nothing could
be done?   0   1   2   3
6. Did you seek or find emotional
social support from loved ones,
friends, or professionals?   0   1   2   3
7. Did you do something with the
specific purpose of relaxing?   0   1   2   3
8. Did you seek or find spiritual or
religious comfort?   0   1   2   3

9. How did you feel that you handled this problem overall? (choose one)
1. Not well at all   2. Not too well   3. OK   4. Fairly well   5.Very well

Health Behaviors Survey
Now we would like you to answer a few questions about your current health.

1. *In the past week, how often did you experience the following feelings? Please choose only one response for each statement.*

	<u>Hardly ever or never</u>	Some of the time	<u>Much or most of time</u>
1. I did not feel like eating: my appetite was poor	0	1	2
2. I felt depressed	0	1	2
3. I felt everything I did was an effort	0	1	2
4. My sleep was restless	0	1	2
5. I was happy	0	1	2
6. I felt lonely	0	1	2
7. People were unfriendly	0	1	2
8. I enjoyed life	0	1	2
9. I felt sad	0	1	2
10. I felt that people disliked me	0	1	2
11. I could not "get going"	0	1	2

2. *For the following statements, please indicate the degree to which you agree or disagree with the following as they apply to **yourself right now**. Choose one response for each statement.*

	Disagree	Strongly Disagree	Agree	Strongly Agree
1. On the whole, I am satisfied with myself.	1	2	3	4
2. I am able to do things as well as most other people.	1	2	3	4
3. I feel that I have a number of good qualities.	1	2	3	4
4. I wish I could have more respect for myself.	1	2	3	4
5. I take a positive attitude toward myself.	1	2	3	4

6. At times I think I am no good at all.			
1	2	3	4
7. All in all, I am inclined to feel that			
I'm a failure. 1	2	3	4
8. I feel that I'm a person of worth,			
at least on an equal plane with others.			
1	2	3	4

ON THE NEXT PAGE, WE WOULD LIKE YOU TO ANSWER SOME

QUESTIONS ABOUT YOUR OWN & YOUR PARENTS'

EXPECTATIONS OF YOU.

Self and Parental Values Survey

Please indicate the extent to which you agree or disagree with the following statements of your feelings of your own and your parents' academic goals and expectations of you. And, we also want to know about your feelings of your relationship with your parent(s). If you don't live with your mother or father and want to describe your relationship with a step-mother or step-father or other parental figure, please answer the following questions with that person in mind.

	Not at all	A little	Some-what	A lot	A great deal
1. How important is it to your parent(s) that you do well in school?	1	2	3	4	5
2. How important is it to your parent(s) that you graduate from high school?	1	2	3	4	5
3. How close are you to your mother?	1	2	3	4	5
4. How important is it to you to graduate from high school?	1	2	3	4	5
5. How important is it to your parent(s) that you get good grades?	1	2	3	4	5
6. How important is it to your parent(s) that you go to college after high school?	1	2	3	4	5
7. How close are you to your father?	1	2	3	4	5
8. How important is it to you that you do well in school?	1	2	3	4	5
9. How important is it to your parent(s) that you get an 'A' on almost every test?	1	2	3	4	5
10. How important is it to your parent(s) that you be one of the best students in your class?	1	2	3	4	5
11. How caring is your mother to you?	1	2	3	4	5

12. How important is it to you that you
get good grades? 1   2   3   4   5

13. How important is it to your parent(s)
that you go to the best college after high
school? 1   2   3   4   5

14. How caring is your father to you? 1   2   3   4   5

15. How important is it to you that you
get an 'A' on almost every test? 1   2   3   4   5

16. How satisfied are you with your
relationship with your mother? 1   2   3   4   5

17. How satisfied are you with your
relationship with your father? 1   2   3   4   5

18. How important is it to you to be one
of the best students in your class? 1   2   3   4   5

19. How important is it to you to go to
the best college after high school? 1   2   3   4   5

20. How much do you feel loved and
wanted by your closest family
members? 1   2   3   4   5

21. How important is it to you to go to
college after high school? 1   2   3   4   5

**ON THE NEXT PAGE, WE WOULD LIKE YOU TO ANSWER SOME
QUESTIONS ABOUT YOUR ETHNIC IDENTITY.**

Ethnic Identity Scale

Please indicate the extent to which you agree or disagree with the following statements of your understanding of your cultural or ethnic identity.

	Not at all	A little	Some- what	A lot	A great deal
1. How often do you speak to your friends in a language other than English?	1	2	3	4	5
2. How proud are you to identify yourself as American?	1	2	3	4	5
3. How often do you speak English to your friends?	1	2	3	4	5
4. How much do you accept White people as close personal friends?	1	2	3	4	5
5. In general, how often do you have positive feelings about White people?	1	2	3	4	5
6. How often can you rely on your own ethnic group for help when you need it?	1	2	3	4	5
7. In general, how often do you have positive feelings about people of your own ethnic group?	1	2	3	4	5
8. How much do you accept people of your own ethnic group as close personal friends?	1	2	3	4	5
9. How much do you appreciate beliefs or values held by those of your own ethnic group?	1	2	3	4	5
10. How much do you like to identify yourself by your own ethnicity?	1	2	3	4	5
11. How often can you count on White friends to be there for you when you need help?	1	2	3	4	5

12. How proud are you to identify
yourself by your own ethnicity?   1   2   3   4   5

13. In general, how knowledgeable are you of
the beliefs & values of the American
culture?   1   2   3   4   5

14. In general, how fluent are you in
your own ethnic language?   1   2   3   4   5

15. How much do you like to identify
yourself as American?   1   2   3   4   5

16. In general, how fluent are you in
English?   1   2   3   4   5

17. How often can you count on friends of
your own ethnic group to be there for you
when you need help?   1   2   3   4   5

18. How often do you speak to your family
in your own ethnic language?   1   2   3   4   5

19. How often can you rely on White people
in general for help when you need it?   1   2   3   4   5

20. How often do you speak English
with your family?   1   2   3   4   5

21. How much do you appreciate beliefs
or values held by White people?   1   2   3   4   5

22. In general, how knowledgeable are you of the
beliefs & values of your own ethnic
group?   1   2   3   4   5

**ON THE NEXT PAGE, WE WOULD LIKE YOU TO ANSWER SOME
QUESTIONS ABOUT YOUR SCHOOL.**

California School Environment Scale

Please indicate the extent to which you agree or disagree with the following statements of your feelings about your school.

	Not at all	A little	Some- what	A lot	A great deal
1. How much do you like this school?	1	2	3	4	5
2. How much is this school helping you get ready for what you want to do after you graduate?	1	2	3	4	5
3. In general, how much do the teachers treat students with respect at your school?	1	2	3	4	5
4. In general, how much do teachers care about students at your school?	1	2	3	4 ·	5
5. How often do you see an academic counselor at your school?	1	2	3	4	5
6. How much are you afraid that someone will hurt or bother you at your school?	1	2	3	4	5
7. How often have you seen a student hit or attack another student at your school?	1	2	3	4	5
8. In general, how much is your ethnic culture celebrated at your school?	1	2	3	4	5
9. In general, how well is your ethnic culture respected at your school?	1	2	3	4	5
10. How clear are you on what you have to do to graduate?	1	2	3	4	5
11. How often are students at your school not treated fairly by other students because of their ethnicity?	1	2	3	4	5
12. How often do you feel uncomfortable at your school because of your ethnicity?	1	2	3	4	5

13. In general, how often do your teachers
give you one-on-one help with your
work? 1 2 3 4 5

14. How often are students at your school
not treated fairly by teachers because of
their ethnicity? 1 2 3 4 5

15. In general, how sensitive are the teachers
to cultural differences at your school? 1 2 3 4 5

16. How much do the different ethnic groups
at your school get along with one
another? 1 2 3 4 5

17. In general, how much do you feel that
your teachers encourage you to continue
your education? 1 2 3 4 5

18. In general, how safe is your school for
your physical well-being? 1 2 3 4 5

19. In general, how much do teachers expect
you to do your best at school? 1 2 3 4 5

20. How often are you afraid that someone
will hit or hurt you because of your
ethnicity? 1 2 3 4 5

21. In general, how much do you respect
your teachers? 1 2 3 4 5

**NOW WE WOULD LIKE TO KNOW YOUR OPINIONS ABOUT WHY
YOU THINK YOUTH STAY IN SCHOOL OR DROP OUT?**

_____
_____
_____
_____

Appendix B

CONSENT TO PARTICIPATE IN A RESEARCH STUDY
UNIVERSITY OF CALIFORNIA, DAVIS

Predictors of Academic Resilience and Persistence in a Cross-Cultural Sample

Principal Investigator:
Rosalva Vargas-Reighley, M.S.
Graduate Student in Human Development

Faculty Supervisor for Ms. Vargas-Reighley:
Carolyn Aldwin, Ph.D.
Human and Community Development

Purpose
You are being asked to participate in a research study. We are studying 600 youths' thoughts and feelings about their values, the school environment, the things they worry about and how they deal with them, and their perceptions of their effectiveness at integrating American and familial cultural values.

Procedures
If you decide to volunteer, you will be asked to fill out a survey, which will take you 1 to 1-1/2 hours. You will be asked to respond to written questions about your thoughts and feelings about your values, the school environment, the things you worry about and how you deal with them, and your perceptions of your effectiveness at integrating American and familial cultural values. There will be one or two research assistants present to answer questions. The survey-taking process will take place in unoccupied classrooms at your school during your elective period.

Risks
There are no expected risks to you for participating in the research study. You may experience some strong feelings during the survey-taking process relating

to the topics being discussed. In the unlikely event that you become distressed because of the survey-taking process, you will be given a referral to see a school counselor.

Participant's initials_____

Benefits

Although there are no direct benefits to you for participating, you may benefit from the opportunity to share your experiences and opinions in the survey-taking process.

Confidentiality

You will be one of several youths participating in the survey-taking process and will be referred to by a name made up by you. The investigator and research assistants will be the only ones with access to this consent form. Your name will not appear on the surveys. However, absolute confidentiality cannot be guaranteed, since research documents are not protected from subpoena.

Costs/Compensation

There is no cost to you beyond the time and effort required for you to participate in the survey-taking process. You will also be compensated $5.00 at the time of the study for your participation.

Right to Refuse or Withdraw

You may refuse to participate in the research study. If you decide to participate, you may also change your mind and quit at any time during the survey-taking process. Also, you may refuse to answer any questions that make you uncomfortable.

Questions

If you have any questions, please ask us. If you have any additional questions later, Rosalva Vargas-Reighley will answer them at the Human Development Department at Hart Hall, University of California, Davis, CA 95616.

Consent

Your signature, below, will indicate that you have decided to participate in the research study and that you have read and understand the information provided above. Please note that you will be given a signed and dated copy of this form to keep. You will also be given a copy of the Experimental Subject's Bill of Rights.

Date: _____   Date: _____

Signature of   Signature of
Respondent: _____   Investigator: _____

Appendix C

CONSENT TO ALLOW YOUR DAUGHTER/SON TO PARTICIPATE IN A RESEARCH STUDY, UNIVERSITY OF CALIFORNIA, DAVIS

Predictors of Academic Resilience in a Cross-Cultural Sample

Principal Investigator:
Rosalva Vargas-Reighley, M.S.
Graduate Student in Human Development

Faculty Supervisor for Ms. Vargas-Reighley:
Carolyn Aldwin, Ph.D.
Human and Community Development

Purpose

You are being asked to allow your daughter or son to participate in a research study. We are studying 600 youths' thoughts and feelings about their values, the school environment, the things they worry about and how they deal with them, and their perceptions of their effectiveness at integrating American and familial cultural values.

Procedures

If you decide that your daughter or son can volunteer, she or he will be asked to fill out a survey, which will take her or him 1 to 1-1/2 hours. Your daughter or son will be asked to respond to written questions about youths' thoughts and feelings about their values, the school environment, the things they worry about and how they deal with them, and their perceptions of their effectiveness at integrating American and familial cultural values. There will be one or two research assistants present to answer questions. The survey-taking process will take place in unoccupied classrooms at your daughters' or sons' school during their elective period.

Risks

There are no expected risks to you for participating in the research study. She or he may experience some strong feelings during the survey-taking process relating to the topics being discussed. In the unlikely event that your daughter of son may become distressed because of the survey-taking process, she or he will be given a referral to see a school counselor.

Participant's initials_____

Benefits

Although there are no direct benefits for your daughter or son for participating, she or he may benefit from the opportunity to share her or his experiences and opinions in the survey-taking process.

Confidentiality

Your daughter or son will be one of several youths participating in the survey-taking process and will be referred to by a name made up by her or him. The investigator and research assistants will be the only ones with access to this consent form. Your daughter or son's name will not appear on the surveys. However, absolute confidentiality cannot be guaranteed, since research documents are not protected from subpoena.

Costs/Compensation

There is no cost to you or your daughter or son beyond the time and effort required for you to participate in the survey-taking process. Your daughter or son will also be compensated $5.00 at the time of the study for her or his participation.

Right to Refuse or Withdraw

You may refuse to allow your daughter or son to participate in the research study. If you decide to allow your daughter or son to participate, you may also change your mind and quit at any time during the survey-taking process. Your daughter or son may also refused to participate, or change her or his mind and quit at any time during the study. Also, your daughter or son may refuse to answer any questions that make her or him uncomfortable.

Questions

If you have any questions, please ask us. If you have any additional questions later, Rosalva Vargas-Reighley will answer them at the Human Development Department at Hart Hall, University of California, Davis, CA 95616.

Consent

Your signature, below, will indicate that you have decided to allow your daughter or son to participate in the research study and that you have read and understand the information provided above. Please note that you will be given a signed and dated copy of this form to keep.

You will also be given a copy of the Experimental Subject's Bill of Rights.

Date and Signature of Parent
Or Guardian:_____

Date and Signature of
Researcher:_____

References

Adler, P. S. (1975). The transitional experience: An alternative view of cultural shock. *Journal of Humanistic Psychology, 15*, 13-23.

Ahearn, F. L. Jr., & Athey, J. L. (1991). *Refugee Children: Theory, Research, and Services*. Baltimore, Maryland: The Johns Hopkins University Press.

Al-Issa, I., Tousignant, M. (1997). *Ethnicity, Immigration, and Psychopathology*. New York: Plenum Press.

Aldwin, C. M., Sutton, K. J., & Lachman, M. (1996). The development of coping resources in adulthood. *Journal of Personality, 64*, 13-23.

Aldwin, C. M. (1994a). *Stress, Coping, and Development: An Integrative Perspective*. New York, NY: Guilford Press.

Aldwin, C.M. (1994b). *The California Coping Inventory*. Paper presented at the annual meeting of the American Psychological Association, Los Angeles.

Aldwin, C., & Greenberger, E. (1987). Cultural differences in the predictors of depression. *American Journal of Community Psychology, 15*, 789-813.

Aldwin, C. M., Levenson, M. R., Spiro III, A., & Bosse, R. (1989). Does emotionality predict stress? Findings from the Normative Aging Study. *Journal of Personality and Social Psychology, 56*(4), 618-624.

Altschuler, J. L., & Ruble, D. N. (1989). Developmental changes in children's awareness of strategies for coping with controllable stress. *Child Development, 60*, 1337-1349.

Alva, S. A., & Padilla, A. M. (1995). Academic invulnerability among Mexican Americans: A conceptual framework. *The Journal of Educational Issues of Language Minority Students, 15*, 27-48.

Alva, S. A. (1993). Differential patterns of achievement among Asian-American adolescents. *Journal of Youth and Adolescence, 22*(4), 407-423.

Alva, S. A. (1991). Academic invulnerability among Mexican-American students: The importance of protective resources and appraisals. *Hispanic Journal of Behavioral Sciences, 13*(1), 18-34.

Arbona, C., & Novy, D. M. (1990). Noncognitive dimensions as predictors of college success among Black, Mexican-American, and White students. *Journal of College Student Development, 31*(5), 415-422.

Arbuckle, J. L. (1995-99). *Amos Version 4.0*. SmallWaters Corporation: Chicago, IL: USA.

Arellano, A. R., & Padilla, A. M. (1996). Academic invulnerability among a select group of Latino university students. *Hispanic Journal of Behavioral Sciences, 18*(4), 485-507.

Astin, A. W. (1977). *Four Critical Years* (1st ed.). S.F.: Jossey-Bass.

Astin, A. W. (1975). *Preventing Students from Dropping Out* (lst ed.). S.F.: Jossey-Bass.

Astin, A. W. (1971). *Predicting Academic Performance in College; Selectivity Data for 2300 American Colleges*. New York: Free Press.

Avalos, M. (1996). Economic restructuring and young Latino workers in the 1980s. In De Anda, R. M. (Ed.), *Chicanas and Chicanos in Contemporary Society*. Needham Heights, MA: Allyn & Bacon.

Baker, S. G. (1996). Demographic trends in the Chicana/o population: Policy implications for the twenty-first century. In Maciel, D. R., & Ortiz, I. D. (Eds.), *Chicanas/Chicanos at the Crossroads: Social, Economic, and Political Change*. Arizona, US: The University of Arizona Press.

Band, E. B. & Weisz, J. R. (1988). How to feel better when if feels bad: Children's perspectives on coping with everyday stress. *Developmental Psychology*, 24, 247-253.

Bandura, A. (1990). Conclusion: Reflections on nonability determinants of competence. In Sternberg, R., and Kolligian, J. Jr. (Eds.), *Competence Considered*. New Haven: Yale University Press, 315-362.

Baumrind, D. (1989). The influence of parenting style on adolescent competence & problem behavior. Paper presented at APA's "*Science Weekend*," New Orleans, August 12-13. Invited address in recognition of the G. Stanley Hall Award conferred by Division 7 in 1988.

Bernard, B. (1991). *Fostering Resiliency in Kids: Protective Factors in the Family, School and Community*. Portland, Oregon: Northwest Regional Educational Laboratory.

Berry, J. W. (1998). Acculturation and Health: Theory and Research. In Kazarian, S. S., & Evans, D. R. (Eds.). *Cultural Clinical Psychology: Theory, Research, and Practice*. New York: Oxford University Press, 39-57.

Berry, J. W. (1992). Acculturation and adaptation in a new society. *International Migration*, 30, 69-85.

Berry, J. W. (1991). Understanding and managing multiculturalism. *Journal of Psychology and Developing Societies*, 3, 17-49.

Berry, J. W. (1990). Psychology of acculturation. In Berman, J. (Ed.), *Nebraska Symposium on Motivation: vol. 37. Cross-Cultural Perspectives* (pp. 201-234). Lincoln: University of Nebraska Press.

Berry, J. W. (1980). Introduction to methodology. In Triandis, H. C., & Berry, J. W. (Eds.), *Handbook of Cross-Cultural Psychology*, Vol. 2. Boston, MA: Allyn & Bacon.

Berry, J. W. (1970). Marginality, stress and ethnic identification in an acculturated Aboriginal community. *Journal of Cross-Cultural Psychology*, 1, 239-252.

Berry, J. W. (1969). On cross-cultural comparability. *International Journal of Psychology*, 4, 119-128.

Billings, A. G., & Moos, R. H. (1981). The role of coping responses and social resources in attenuating the stress of life events. *Journal of Behavioral Medicine*, 4, 139-157.

Blair, S. L., & Qian, Z. (1998). Family and Asian students' educational performance: A consideration of diversity. *Journal of Family Issues*, 19(4), 355-374.

Bromley, M. A. (1988). Identity as a central issue for the Southeast Asian unaccompanied refugee minor. *Child & Youth Care Quarterly*, 17(2), 104-114.

Bronfenbrenner, U. (1986). Ecology of family as a context for human development: Research perspectives. *Developmental Psychology*, 22, 723-742.

Brown, J. M., O'Keeffe, J., Sanders, S. H., & Baker, B. (1986). Developmental changes in children's cognition to stressful and painful situations. *Journal of Pediatric Psychology*, 11, 343-357.

Brown, W. F., & Holtzman, W. H. (1967). *Survey of Study Habits and Attitudes*. New York: Psychological Corporation.

Buenning, M., & Toolefson, N. (1987). Cultural gap hypothesis an explanation for achievement patterns of Mexican-American students. *Psychology in the Schools*, 24, 264-271.

Burbach, D. J., & Borduin, C. M. (1986). Parent-child relations and the etiology of depression: A review of methods and findings. *Clinical Psychology Review*, 6, 133-153.

Buriel, R., Perez, W., De Ment, T. L., Chavez, D. V., & Moran, V. R. (1998). The relationship of language brokering to academic performance, biculturalism, and self-efficacy among Latino adolescents. *Hispanic Journal of Behavioral Sciences*, 20(3), 283-297.

Buriel, R. (1993). Acculturation, respect for cultural differences and biculturalism among three generations of Mexican American and Euro American school children. *Journal of Genetic Psychology*, 4, 531-543.

Buriel, R., & Cardoza, D. (1988). Sociocultural correlates of achievement among three generations of Mexican American high school seniors. *American Educational Research Journal*, 25(2), 177-192.

Buriel, R., Calzada, S., & Vasquez, R. (1982). The relationship of traditional Mexican American culture to adjustment and delinquency among three generations of Mexican American male adolescents. *Hispanic Journal of Behavioral Sciences*, 4(1), 41-55.

Buriel, R., & Luu, N. T. (1993). *The Relationship of Biculturalism and Parents' Aspirations to Vietnamese- and Mexican American High School Students' Academic Achievement and Aspirations*. Unpublished manuscript, Pomona College, Psychology Department, Claremont, CA.

Calabrese, R. L., & Poe, J. (1990). Alienation: An explanation of high dropout rates among African American and Latino Students. *Educational Research Quarterly*, 12(4), 22-26.

Cervantes, R. C., & Castro, F. G. (1985). Stress, coping, and Mexican American mental health: A systematic review. *Hispanic Journal of Behavioral Sciences*, 7, 1-73.

Chao, C. M. (1992). The inner heart: Therapy with Southeast Asian families. In Vargas, L. A., & Koss-Chioino, J. D. (Eds.), *Working with Culture: Psychotherapeutic Interventions with Ethnic Minority Children and Adolescents*. San Francisco: Jossey-Bass.

Chapa, J., & Valencia, R. R. (1993). Latino population growth, demographic characteristics, and educational stagnation: An examination of recent trends. *Hispanic Journal of Behavioral Sciences*, 15, 165-187.

Children's Defense Fund (1991). *The State of America's Children*. Washington, DC.

Chun, K. M., Balls Organista, P., & Marín, G. (2003). *Acculturation: Advances in Theory, Measurement, and Applied Research*. Washington, DC: American Psychological Association.

Cohen, F. (1984). Coping. In Matarazzo, J., Weiss, S., Herd, J., Miller, N., & Weiss, S. (Eds.), *Behavioral Health: A Handbook of Health Enhancement and Disease Prevention*. New York: Wiley.

Cohen, J., & Cohen, P. (1983). *Applied Multiple Regression/Correlation Analysis for the Behavioral Sciences (2nd ed.)*. Hillsdale, NJ: Lawrence Erlbaum Associates.

Cohen, S., & Wills, T. A. (1985). Stress, social support, and the buffering hypothesis. *Psychological Bulletin*, 98, 310-357.

Compas, B. E. (1992). *Promoting Successful Coping During Adolescence*. Paper presented at the conference, Youth in the Year 2000: Psychological Issues and Interventions, Marbach Castle, Germany, November.

Compas, B. E., & Wagner, B. M. (1991). Psychological stress during adolescence: Intrapersonal and interpersonal processes. In M. E. Colten & S. Gore (Eds.), *Adolescent Stress: Causes and Consequences* (pp. 67-86). New York: Aldine de Gruyter.

Compas, B. E. (1987). Coping with stress during childhood and adolescence. *Psychological Bulletin*, 101(3), 393-403.

Compas, B. E., Davis, G. E., & Forsythe, C. J. (1985). Characteristics of life events during adolescence. *American Journal of Community Psychology*, 13, 677-691.

Compas, B. E., Forsythe, C. J., & Wagner, B. M. (1988). Consistency and variability in causal attributions and coping with stress. *Cognitive Therapy and Research*, 12(3), 305-320.

Compas, B. E., Malcarne, B. L., & Fondacaro, K. M. (1988). Coping with stressful events in older children and young adolescents. *Journal of Consulting and Clinical Psychology*, 56(3), 405-411.

Compas, B. E., Orosan, P. G., & Grant, K. E. (1993). Adolescent stress and coping: Implications for psychopathology during adolescence. *Journal of Adolescence*, 16, 33-39.

Compas, B. E., Worsham, N. L., & Ey, S. (1992). Conceptual and developmental issues in children's coping with stress. In La Greca, A. M., Siegel, L. J., Wallander, J. L., & Walker, C. E. (Eds.), *Stress and Coping in Child Health* (pp. 7-24). New York: Guilford Press.

Cope, R. & Hannah, W. (1975). *Revolving College Doors: The Causes and Consequences of Dropping Out, Stopping, and Transferring.* New York: Wiley.

Craen, H. F. (1994). *Adjustment in Hispanic Middle School Students: An Integrative Model of Risk and Protective Factors.* Unpublished doctoral dissertation, University of Texas at Austin.

Cramer, D. (1994). *Introducing Statistics for Social Research: Step-by-Step Calculations and Computer Techniques Using SPSS.* New York, N.Y.: Routledge.

Cuellar, I., Harris, L. C., & Jasso, R. (1980). An acculturation scale for Mexican American normal and clinical populations. *Hispanic Journal of Behavioral Sciences, 2,* 199-217.

Curry, S. L., & Russ, S. W. (1985). Identifying coping strategies in children. *Journal of Clinical Child Psychology, 14,* 61-69.

Darder, A., Torres, R. D., & Gutierrez, H. (1997). *Latinos and Education: A Critical Reader.* New York, NY: Routledge.

Davidson, G. R., Nurcombe, B., Kearney, G. E., & Davis, K. (1978). Culture, conflict and coping in a group of Aboriginal adolescents. *Culture, Medicine and Psychiatry, 2,* 359-372.

De Anda, R. M. (1996). *Chicanas and Chicanos in Contemporary Society.* Needham Heights, MA: Allyn & Bacon.

De La Rosa, D., & Maw, C. (1990). *Hispanic Education: A Statistical Portrait 1990.* Washington, D.C.: National Council of La Raza.

Der-Karabetian, A., & Ruiz, Y. (1997). Affective bicultural and global-human identity scales for Mexican-American adolescents. *Psychological Reports, 80,* 1027-1039.

Deyo, R. A., Diehl, A. K., Hazuda, H., & Stern, M. P. (1985). A simple language-based acculturation scale for Mexican Americans: Validation and application to health care research. *American Journal of Public Health, 75,* 51-55.

Donato, R., Menchaca, M., & Valencia, R. R. (1991). Segregation, desegregation, and integration of Chicano students: Problems and porspects. In: Valencia, R. R. (Ed.), *Chicano School Failure and Success: Research and Policy Agendas for the 1990s.* (The Stanford Series on Education and Public Policy). Basingstoke, England: Falmer Press.

DoungTran, Q., Lee, S., & Khoi, S. (1996). Ethnic and gender differences in parental expectations and life stress. *Child and Adolescent Social Work Journal, 13(6),* 515-526.

Downey, G., & Coyne, J. C. (1990). Children of depressed parents: An integrative review. *Psychological Bulletin, 108,* 50-76.

Dryfoos, J. G. (1990). *Adolescent at Risk: Prevalence and Prevention.* New York: Oxford University Press.

Eckensberger, L. (1972). The necessity of a theory for applied cross-cultural research. In Cronbach, L. J. C., Drenth, P. J. D. (Eds.), *Mental Tests and Cultural Adaptation.* (pp. 99-107). The Hague: Mouton.

Elder, G. H., Jr. (1974). *Children of the Great Depression.* Chicago: University of Chicago Press.

Egeland, B., Breitenbucher, M., & Rosenberg, D. (1980). Prospective study of the significance of life stress in the etiology of child abuse. *Journal of Consulting and Clincial Psychology, 48,* 195-205.

Epstein, J., & Karweit, N. (1983). *Friends in School: Patterns of Selection and Influence in Secondary Schools.* New York: Academic Press.

Folkman, S., & Lazarus, R. S. (1980). An analysis of coping in a middle-aged community sample. *Journal of Health and Social Behavior, 21,* 219-239.

Fordham, S., & Ogbu, J. U. (1986). Black students school success: Coping with the burden of 'acting white'. *Urban Review, 18,* 176-206.

Fratoe, F. A. (1981). The education of nonmetro Hispanics. *The Education Digest,* 43-45.

Fuligni, A. J. (1997). The academic achievement of adolescents from immigrant families: The roles of family background, attitudes, and behavior. *Child Development, 68*(2), 351-363.

Furnham, A. & Bochner, S. (1986). *Culture Shock: Psychological Reactions to Unfamiliar Environments.* London: Methuen.

Gandara, P. (1995). *Over the Ivy Walls: The Educational Mobility of Low-Income Chicanos.* Albany, N.Y.: State University of New York Press.

Garmezy, N. (1985). Stress-resistant children: The search for protective factors. In Steveson, J. E. (Ed.), *Recent Research in Developmental Psychopathology. Journal of Child Psychology and Psychiatry* (Book Supplement No. 4), 213-233.

Garmezy, N., Masten, A. S., & Tellegen, A. (1984). The study of stress and competence in children: A building block for developmental psychopathology. *Child Development, 55,* 97-111.

Ge, X., Conger, R. D., Lorenz, F. O., Shanahan, M., & Elder, G. H., Jr. (1995). Mutual influences in parent and adolescent psychological distress. *Developmental Psychology, 31,* 406-419.

Gibson, M. (1993). Variability in immigrant students' school performance: The U.S. case. *Division G Newsletter,* Winter. Washington, D.C.: American Educational Research Association.

Gibson, M. A., & Ogbu, J. U. (1991). *Minority Status and Schooling: A Comparative Study of Immigrant and Involuntary Minorities.* New York: Garland.

Giggs, J. A. (1977). The mental health of immigrants in Australia. In Bowen, M. (Ed.), *Australia 2000: The Ethnic Impact.* Armidale, N.S.W.: University of New England Publishing Unit.

Gonzalez, R., & Padilla, A. M. (1998). *School Context and Social Support as Predictors of Academic Achievement among Mexican American Students.* Paper presented at the annual meeting of the American Educational Research Assn. San Diego, California.

Gonzalez, R., & Padilla, A. M. (1997). The academic resilience of Mexican American high school students. *Hispanic Journal of Behavioral Sciences,* 19, 301-317.

Goodenow, C. (1992). *School Motivation, Engagement, and Sense of Belonging among Urban Adolescent Students.* (ERIC Document Reproduction Service No. 349 364).

Goodman, M. E. (1964). *Race Awareness in Young Children* (revised ed.). New York: Collier (Original publication, 1952).

Gore, S., & Eckenrode, J. (1996). Context and process in research on risk and resilience. In: Haggerty, R. J., Sherrod, L. R., Garmezy, N., & Rutter, M. *Stress, Risk, and Resilience in Children and Adolescents: Processes, Mechanisms, and Interventions.* New York, NY: Cambridge University Press.

Graves, T. (1967). Psychological acculturation in a tri-ethnic community. *South-Western Journal of Anthropology,* 23, 337-350.

Greco, T., Vasta, E., & Smith, R. (1977). "I get these freaky feelings like I'm splitting into a million pieces." Cultural differences in Brisbane, Australia. *Ethnic Studies,* 1, 17-29.

Gross, E. (1970). Work, organization, and stress. In Levine, S., & Scotch, N. A. (Eds.), *Social Stress* (pp. 54-110). Chicago: Aldine.

Gutierrez, D. G. (1995). *Walls and Mirrors: Mexican Americans, Mexican Immigrants, and the Politics of Ethnicity.* Berkeley, CA: University of California Press.

Haggerty, R. J., Sherrod, L. R., Garmezy, N., Rutter, M. (1996). *Stress, Risk, and Resilience in Children and Adolescents: Processes, Mechanisms, and Interventions.* New York, NY: Cambridge University Press.

Harrison, A. O., Wilson, M., Pine, C. J., Chan, S., & Buriel, R. (1990). Family ecologies of ethnic minority children. *Child Development,* 61, 347-367.

Hernandez, L. P. (1993). *The Role of Protective Factors in the School Resilience of Mexican American High School Students.* Unpublished doctoral dissertation, Stanford University, Stanford, CA.

Hernandez, N. G. (1973). Variables affecting achievement of middle school Mexican American students. *Review of Educational Research,* 43(1), 1-39.

Hernandez-Chavez, E. (1984). The inadequacy of English Immersion Education as an educational approach for language minority students in the United States. In: *Studies on Immersion Education.* Sacramento: California State Department of Education.

Hirano-Nakanishi, M. (1986). The extent and relevance of pre-high school attrition and delayed education for Hispanics. *Hispanic Journal of Behavioral Sciences,* 8(1), 61-76.

Holahan, C. J., Moos, R. H. (1994). Life stressors and mental health: Advances in conceptualizing stress resistance. In Avison, W. R., & Gotlib, I. H. (Eds.), *Stress and Mental Health: Contemporary Issues and Prospects for the Future*. New York: Plenum Press.

Holahan, C. J., & Moos, R. H. (1991). Life stressors, personal and social resources, and depression: A 4-year structural model. *Journal of Abnormal Psychology*, 100, 31-38.

Holahan, C. J., Valentiner, D. P., & Moos, R. H. (1995). Parental support, coping strategies, and psychological adjustment: An integrative model with late adolescents. *Journal of Youth and Adolescence*, 24(6), 633-648.

Huang, L. H. (1998). Southeast Asian refugee children and adolescents. In: Gibbs, J. T., & Huang, L. N. *Children of Color: Psychological Interventions with Culturally Diverse Youth*. San Francisco. CA: Jossey-Bass.

Ianni, F. A. J. & Orr, M. T. (1996). Dropping out. In Graber, J. A., Brooks-Gunn, J., & Petersen, A. C. (Eds.). *Transitions Through Adolescence: Interpersonal Domains and Context*. Mahwah, New Jersey: Lawrence Erlbaum Assn.

Ianni, F. A. J. (1989). *The Search for Structure: A Report on American Youth Today*. New York: The Free Press.

James, L. R., Mulaik, S. A., & Brett, J. M. (1982). *Causal Analysis: Assumptions, Models, and Data*. Beverly Hills, CA: Sage.

Johnston, R. (1972). *Future Australians: Immigrant Children in Perth, Western Australia*. Canberra: Australian National University Press.

Kao, G., & Tienda, M. (1998). Educational aspirations of minority youth. *American Journal of Education*, 106, 349-384.

Keefe, S. E., & Padilla, A. M. (1987). *Chicano Ethnicity*. Albuquerque: University of New Mexico Press.

Kiefer, C. (1974). *Changing Cultures, Changing Lives*. San Francisco: Jossey-Bass.

Kimball, W. L. (1968). Parent and family influences on academic achievement among Mexican-American students (Doctoral dissertation, University of California, Los Angeles). *Dissertation Abstracts International,* 29, 1965A. (University Microfilms No. 68-16,550).

Kinzie, J. D. (1993). Posttraumatic effects and their treatment among Southeast Asian refugees. In Wilson, J. P., & Raphael, B. (Eds.), *International Handbook of Traumatic Stress Syndromes*. New York: Plenum Press.

Kiresuk, T. J., & Sherman, R. E. (1968). Goal attainment scaling: A general method for evaluating comprehensive community mental health programs. *Community Mental Health Journal*, 4, 443-453.

Kirsch, I. S., & Jungeblut, A. (1986). *Literacy: Profiles of America's Young Adults, National Assessment of Educational Progress, Report 16-P1-01*. Princeton, NJ: Educational Testing Service.

Kohut, H. (1971). *The Analysis of the Self*. New Haven, CT: Yale University Press.

Kulka, R., Kahle, L., & Klingel, D. (1982). Aggression, deviance, and personality adaption as antecedents and consequences of alienation and involvement in high school. *Journal of Youth and Adolescence*, 11, 261-279.

Kourakis, M. (1983). *Biculturalism: The Effect upon Personal and Social Adjustment.* Master's thesis, University of Adelaide.

LaFromboise, T., Coleman, H.L.K., & Gerton, J. (1993). Psychological impact of biculturalism: evidence and theory. *Psychological Bulletin*, 114(3), 395-412.

Landsman, M. A., Padilla, A. M., Leiderman, P. H., Clark, C., Ritter, P., & Dornbusch, S. (1992). *Biculturalism and Academic Achievement among Asian and Hispanic Adolescents.* Unpublished manuscript, Stanford University, School of Education, Palo Alto, CA.

Lango, D. R. (1995). Mexican American female enrollment in graduate programs: A study of the characteristics that may predict success. *Hispanic Journal of Behavioral Sciences.* 1(17), 33-48.

Lazarus, R. S., & Folkman, S. (1984). *Stress, Appraisal, and Coping.* New York: Springer.

Lerner, R. M., Lerner, J. V., von Eye, A., Ostrom, C. W., Nitz, K., Talwar-Soni, R., & Tubman, J. G. (1996). Continuity and discontinuity across the transition of early adolescence: A developmental contextual perspective. In Graber, J. A., Brooks-Gunn, J., & Petersen, A. C. (Eds.). *Transitions Through Adolescence: Interpersonal Domains and Context.* Mahwah, New Jersey: Lawrence Erlbaum.

Lerner, J. V., & Vicary, J. R. (1984). Difficult temperament and drug use: Analyses from the New York longitudinal study. *Journal of Drug Education*, 14, 1-8.

Lese, K. P., & Robbins, S. B. (1994). Relationship between goal attributes and the academic achievement of Southeast Asian adolescent refugees. *Journal of Counseling Psychology*, 41(1), 45-52.

LeShan, E. J. (1997). In Maggio, R. *Quotations on Education.* Paramus, New Jersey: Prentice Hall.

Lewin, K. (1948). Self-hatred in Jews. In Lewin, K. (Ed.), *Resolving Social Conflicts*, 186-200. New York: Harper.

Leyva, W. L. (1990). Acculturation, social support, and coping as mediators of stress among Mexican women. *Dissertation Abstracts International*.

Looff, D. (1979). Sociocultural factors in etiology. In Noshpitz, J. D. (Ed.), *Basic Handbook of Child Psychiatry* (Vol. 2, pp. 87-99). New York: Basic Books.

Marin, G., & Marin Van Oss, B. (1991). *Research with Hispanic Populations.* Newbury Park, CA: Sage Publications.

Marin, G., Sabogal, F., Marin, B. V., Otero-Sabogal, R., & Perez-Stable, E. J. (1987). Development of a short acculturation scale for Hispanics. *Hispanic Journal of Behavioral Sciences*, 9, 183-205.

Mason, J. W. (1975). A historical view of the stress field. *Journal of Human Stress*, 1, 6-27.

Matsuoka, J. (1991). "Vietnamese Americans." In: Mokuau, N. (ed.), *Handbook of Social Services for Asian and Pacific Islanders*. Westport, Conn.: Greenwood Press.

Matsuoka, J. K. (1990). Differential acculturation among Vietnamese refugees. *Social Work*, 35, 341-345.

Mattlin, J., Wethington, E., & Kessler, R. C. (1990). Situational determinants of coping and coping effectiveness. *Journal of Health and Social Behavior*, 31, 103-122.

Mehan, H., Hubbard, L., & Villanueva, I. (1994). Forming academic identities: Accommodation without assimilation among involuntary minorities. *Anthropology and Education Quarterly*, 25, 91-117.

Meichenbaum, D. (1985). *Stress Inoculation Training*. New York: Pergamon Press.

Mena, F. J., Padilla, A. M., & Maldonado, M. (1987). Acculturative stress and specific coping stategies among immigrant and later generation college students. *Hispanic Journal of Behavioral Sciences*, 9(2), 207-225.

Moos, R. H., & Billings, A. G. (1982). Conceptualizing and measuring coping resources and processes. In Goldberger, L., & Breznitz, S. (Eds.), *Handbook of Stress: Theoretical and Clinical Aspects.* (pp. 212-230). New York: Fress Press.

Mussen, P. H. (1953). Differences between the TAT responses of Negro and White boys. *Journal of Consulting Psychology*, 17, 373-376.

National Center for Education Statistics. (1995). *Dropout Rates in the United States: 1995.* (U.S. Department of Education, Office of Educational Research and Improvement). Washington, DC: U.S. Government Printing Office.

National Center for Education Statistics (1994). {Unpublished materials}. Washington, DC: Department of Education.

National Center for Education Statistics (1993). *Losing Generations: Adolescents in High Risk Settings*. Washington, DC: National Academy Press.

National Center for Education Statistics. (1992). *Language Characteristics and Academic Achievement: A Look at Asian and Hispanic Eighth Graders in the National Education Longitudinal Study of 1988 (NELS: 88)*. (U.S. Department of Education, Office of Educational Research and Improvement). Washington, DC: U.S. Government Printing Office.

National Council of La Raza (1992). *State of Hispanic America 1991: An Overview*. Washington, D.C.: Author.

The National Education Goals Report. (1991). *Building a Nation of Learners*. Washington, DC: National Education Goals Panel.

National Education Longitudinal Study (NELS) (1988). (Unpublished data). U.S. Department of Education, National Center for Education Statistics.

National Research Council (1993). *Losing Generations: Adolescents in High Risk Settings*. Washington, DC: National Academy Press.

Nettles, S. M., & Pleck, J. H. (1996). Risk, resilience, and development: The multiple ecologies of black adolescents in the United States. In: Haggerty, R. J., Sherrod, L. R., Garmezy, N., & Rutter, M., *Stress, Risk, and Resilience in Children and Adolescents: Processes, Mechanisms, and Interventions.* New York, NY: Cambridge University Press.

Nicassio, P. M. (1985). The psychosocial adjustment of the South-east Asian refugee. *Journal of Cross-Cultural Psychology,* 16, 153-173.

Nicassio, P. M., Solmon, G. S., Guest, S. S., & McCallough, J. E. (1986). Emigration stress and language proficiency as correlates of depression in a sample of Southeast Asian refugees. *International Journal of Social Psychiatry,* 32, 22-28.

Nicholson, B. L. (1997). The influence of pre-emigration and post-emigration stressors on mental health: A study of Southeast Asian refugees. *Social Work Research,* 21(1), 19-31.

Nielsen, F., & Fernandez, R. M. (1981). *Hispanic Students in American High Schools: Background Characteristics and Achievement.* Washington, DC: National Center for Education Statistics.

Nishio, K., & Bilmes, M. (1998). Psychotherapy with Southeast Asian American clients. In Atkinson, D. R., Morten, G., & Sue, D. W. (Eds.), *Counseling American Minorities* (5th ed.). San Francisco: McGraw-Hill.

Ogbu, J. U. (1978). *Minority Education and Caste: The American System in Cross-Cultural Perspective.* New York: Academic Press.

Olmedo, E. L. (1979). Acculturation: A psychometric perspective. *American Psychologist,* 34, 1061-1070.

Olmedo, E. L., & Padilla, A. M. (1978). Empirical and construct validation of a measure of acculturation for Mexican Americans. *The Journal of Social Psychology,* 105, 179-187.

Ong, P., & Hee, Suzanne, J. (1993). The growth of the Asian Pacific American population: Twenty million in 2020. In: *The State of Asian Pacific America: A Public Policy Report.* Los Angeles: LEAP Asian Pacific American Public Policy Institute and UCLA Asian American Studies Center, 11-24.

Orum, L. S. (1986). *The Education of Hispanics: Status and Implications.* Washington, D.C.: National Council of La Raza.

Padilla, A. M. (1994). Bicultural development: A theoretical and empirical examination. In Malgady, R. G., & Rodriguez, O. (Eds.), *Theoretical and Conceptual Issues in Hispanic Mental Health.* Malabar, Florida: Krieger.

Padilla, A. M. (1980). *Acculturation: Theory, Models and Some New Findings.* Boulder, Colorado: Westview Press.

Pantages, T. J. & Creedon, C. F. (1978). Studies of college attrition: 1950-1975. *Review of Educational Research.* Winter, 48(1), 49-101.

Paz, O. (1959). *El Laberinto de la Soledad* (2nd ed.). Mexico, D.F.: Fondao de Cultura Economico.

Perez, S. M. & Salazar De La Rosa, D. (1997). Economic, Labor Force, and Social Implications of Latino Educational and Population Trends. In Darder, A., Torres, R. D., & Gutierrez, H. (Eds.), *Latinos and Education: A Critical Reader*. New York: Routledge.

Perez, S. M. & Duany, L. (1992). *Reducing Hispanic Teenage and Family Poverty: A Replication Guide*. Washington, DC: National Council of La Raza.

Petersen, A. C., & Hamburg, B. A. (1986). Adolescence: A developmental approach to problems in psychopathology. *Behavior Therapy*, 17, 480-499.

Phinney, J. S. (1993). A three-stage model of ethnic identity development in adolescence. In Bernal, M. E., & Knight, G. P. (Eds.). *Ethnic Identity: Formation and Transmission among Hispanics and Other Minorities*. Albany, NY: State University of New York Press.

Pho, L. T. (1994). *Family Education and Academic Performance among Southeast Asian Students*. Dissertation.

Porte, Z., & Torney-Purta, J. (1987). Depression and academic achievement among Indochinese refugee unaccompanied minors in ethnic and nonethnic placements. *American Journal of Orthopsychiatry*, 57, 536-547.

Radloff, L. S. (1977). The CES D scale: A self-report depression scale for research in the general population. *Applied Psychological Measurement*, 1, 385-401.

Ramirez, M. III. (1998). *Multicultural/Multiracial Psychology: Mestizo Perspectives in Personality and Mental Health*. Northvale, New Jersey: Jason Aronson Inc.

Ramirez, M. III (1984). Assessing and understanding biculturalism-multiculturalism in Mexican-American adults. In Martinez, J. L. & Mendoza, R. H. (Eds.). *Chicano Psychology*. San Diego, CA: Academic Press.

Ramirez, M. III (1983). *Psychology of the Americas*. New York: Pergamon.

Ramirez, M. III, & Castaneda, A. (1974). *Cultural Democracy, Bicognitve Development and Education*. New York: Academic Press.

Ramirez, M. III, & Price-Williams, D. (1974). Cognitive styles of children in three ethnic groups in the U.S. *Journal of Cross-Cultural Psychology*, 5, 212-219.

Reimers, D. M. (1985). *Still the Golden Door: The Third World Comes to America*. New York: Columbia University Press.

Reyes, P., & Valencia, R. R. (1993). Educational policy and the growing Latino student population: Problems and prospects. *Hispanic Journal of Behavioral Sciences*, 15, 258-283.

Rochin, R. I., & Castillo, M. D. (1993). *Immigration, Colonia Formation, and Latino Poor in Rural California: Evolving "Immiseration"* (Occasional Paper Series, No. 93-1). Los Angeles: The Tomas Rivera Center.

Rogler, L. H., Cortes, D. E., & Malgady, R. G. (1991). Acculturation and mental health status among Hispanics. *American Psychologist*, 46, 585-597.

Rosenberg, M. (1965). *Society and the Adolescent Self-Image.* Princeton, New Jersey: Princeton University Press.

Rosenthal, D. (1987). Ethnic identity development in adolescents. In Phinney, J. & Rotheram, M. (Eds.), *Children's Ethnic Socialization: Pluralism and Development,* 156-179. Beverly Hills, CA: Sage Publications.

Rotheram-Borus, M. J. (1993). Biculturalism among adolescents. In Bernal, M. E., & Knight, G. P. (Eds.), *Ethnic Identity: Formation and Transmission among Hispanics and Other Minorities.* Albany, NY: State University of New York Press.

Rotheram-Borus, M. (1989). Ethnic differences in adolescents' identity status and associated behavior problems. *Journal of Adolescence,* 12, 361-374.

Rumbaut, R. G. (2000). Profiles in resilience: Educational achievement and ambition among children of immigrants in Southern California. In Taylor, R. D., & Wang, M. C. (Eds.), *Resilience Across Contexts: Family, Work, Culture, and Community.* Mahwah, New Jersey: Lawrence Erlbaum Ass.

Rumberger, R. W. (1991). Chicano dropouts: A review of research and policy issues. In: Valencia, R. R. (Ed.), *Chicano School Failure and Success: Research and Policy Agendas for the 1990s.* (The Stanford Series on Education and Public Policy). Baskingstoke, England: Falmer Press, 64-89.

Rutter, M. (1987). Psychosocial resilience and protective mechanisms. *American Journal of Orthopsychiatry,* 57, 316-331.

Rutter, M. (1985). Resilience in the face of adversity: Protective factors and resistance to psychiatric disorder. *British Journal of Psychiatry,* 147, 598-611.

Rutter, M., & Quinton, D. (1984). Long-term follow-up of women institutionalized in childhood: Factors promoting good functioning in adult life. *British Journal of Developmental Psychology,* 18, 225-234.

Rutter, M. (1980). *Changing Youth in a Changing Society.* Cambridge, MA: Harvard University Press.

Rutter, M. (1979). Protective factors in children's responses to stress and disadvantage. In N. Kent & Ray (eds.), *Primary Prevention of Psychopathology, Vol. 3: Social Competence in Children.* Hanover, New Hampshire: University Press of New England, 49-74.

Salgado de Snyder, N. (1987). Factors associated with acculturation stress and depressive symptomatology among married Mexican immigrant women. *Psychology of Women Quarterly,* 11, 475-488.

Schaefer, C., Coyne, J. C., & Lazarus, R. (1981). The health-related function of social support. *Journal of Behavioral Medicine,* 4, 381-405.

Schumaker, P. D., & Getter, R. W. (1977). The community bases of minority educational attainment. *Journal of Education,* 159, 5-22.

Simonton, D. K. (1987). Developmental antecedents of achieved imminence. *Annals of Child Development,* 4, 131-169.

Smith, T. M. (1995). *The Condition of Education.* National Center for Education Statistics. U.S. Dept. of Education.

So, A. (1987). High-achieving disadvantaged students: A study of low SES Hispanic language minority youth. *Urban Education*, 22(1), 19-35.

Sokoloff, B., Carlin, J., & Pham, H. (1984). Five year follow up of Vietnamese refugee children in the United States: Part 1. *Clinical Pediatrics*, 23, 565-570.

Solberg, V. S., & Villarreal, P. (1997). Examination of self-efficacy, social support, and stress as predictors of psychological and physical distress among Hispanic college students. *Hispanic Journal of Behavioral Sciences*, 19(2), 182-201.

Solberg, V. S., Valdez, J., & Villareal, P. (1994). Social support, stress, and Hispanic college adjustment: Test of a Diathesis-Stress model. *Hispanic Journal of Behavioral Sciences*, 16(3), 230-239.

Stanton-Salazar, R. D. (1997). A social capital framework for understanding the socialization of racial minority children and youths. *Harvard Educational Review*, 67(1), 1-40.

Stanton-Salazar, R. D., & Dornbusch, S. M. (1995). Social capital and the reproduction of inequality: Information networks among Mexican-origin high school students. *Sociology of Education*, 68, 116-135.

Stark, L. J., Spirito, A., Williams, C. A., & Guevremont, D. C. (1989). Common problems and coping strategies I: Findings with normal adolescents. *Journal of Abnormal Child Psychology*, 17(2), 203-212.

Steinberg, L., Brown, B., Cider, M., Kaczmarck, N., & Lazzaro, C. (1988). *Noninstructional Influences on High School Student Achievement: The Contributions of Parents, Peers, Extracurricular Activities, and Part-time Work*. Madison, Wisconsin: National Center on Effective Secondary Schools.

Steinberg, L., Dornbusch, S. M., Brown, B. B. (1992). Ethnic differences in adolescent achievement. *American Psychologist*, 47(6), 723-729.

Stone, A. A., & Neale, J. M. (1984). New measure of daily coping: Development and preliminary results. *Journal of Personality and Social Psychology*, 46, 892-906.

Stonequist, E. (1935). The problem of a marginal man. *American Journal of Sociology*, 41, 1-12.

Suarez, S. A., Fowers, B. J., Garwood, C. S., & Szapocznik, J. (1997). Biculturalism, differentness, loneliness, and alienation in Hispanic college students. *Hispanic Journal of Behavioral Sciences*, 19(4), 489-505.

Suárez-Orozco, C. & Suárez-Orozco, M. (1995). *Transformations: Migration, Family Life, and Achievement Motivation among Latino Adolescents*. Stanford, CA: Stanford University Press.

Sue, S., & Okazaki, S. (1990). Asian American educational achievements: A phenomenon in search of an explanation. *American Psychologist*, 45, 913-920.

Sue, S., Sue, D. W., Sue, L., Takeuchi, D. T. (1995). Psychopathology among Asian Americans: A model minority? *Cultural Diversity and Mental Health*, 1(1), 39-51.

Suinn, R., Rickard-Figueroa, K., Lew, S., & Vigil, P. (1987). The Suinn-Lew Asian Self-Identity Acculturation Scale: An initial report. *Educational and Psychological Measurement*, 47, 401-407.

Szapocznik, J., & Kurtines, W. M. (1980). Acculturation, biculturalism, and adjustment among Cuban Americans. In Padilla, A. M. (Ed.), *Recent Advances in Acculturation Research: Theory, Models and Some New Findings.* Boulder, CO: Westview, 139-161.

Szapocznik, J., Kurtines, W. M., & Fernandez, T. (1980). Bicultural involvement and adjustment in Hispanic-American youths. *International Journal of Intercultural Relations*, 4, 353-365.

Szapocznik, J., Scopetta, M. A., Kurtines, W., & Aranalde, M. A. (1978). Theory and measurement of acculturation. *Interamerican Journal of Psychology*, 12, 113-130.

Taft, R. (1977). Coping with unfamiliar cultures. In Warren, N. (Ed.), *Studies in Cross-Cultural Psychology.* London: Academic Press.

Trimble, J. E. (2003). Introduction: Social change and acculturation. In Chun, K. M., Balls Organista, P., & Marín, G. (Eds.), *Acculturation: Advances in Theory, Measurement, and Applied Research.* Washington, DC: American Psychological Association.

Triandis, H. C. (1995). *Individualism & Collectivism.* Boulder, Colorado: Westview Press.

Triandis, H. C., Kashima, Y., Hui, H. C., Lisansky, J., & Marin, G. (1982). Acculturation and biculturalism indexes among relatively acculturate Hispanic young adults. *Interamerican Journal of Psychology*, 16, 140-149.

Triandis, H. C., Malpass, R. S., & Davidson, A. (1972). Cross-cultural psychology. *Biennial Review of Anthropology.*

Turner, R. (1968). The self-conception in social interaction. In Gordon, C. & Gergen, K. (Eds.), *The Self in Social Interaction.* New York: Wiley.

U.S. Bureau of the Census. (1995). *The Nation's Asian and Pacific Islander Population, 1994.* Washington, D.C.: U.S. Dept. of Commerce.

U.S. Commission on Civil Rights (1992). *Civil Rights Issues Facing Asian Americans in the 1990's.* Washington, DC: Author.

U.S. Department of Health and Human Services. (1987). *Refugee Resettlement Program: Report to the Congress.* Washington, DC: U.S. Department of Health and Human Services.

Valencia, A. A. (1994). The attributes of academically successful Mexican-American university male and female students. *Journal of Multicultural Counseling and Development*, 22, 215-226.

Valencia, R. R. (1991). *Chicano School Failure and Success: Research and Policy Agendas for the 1990s.* (The Stanford Series on Education and Public Policy). Basingstoke, England: Falmer Press.

Valencia, R. R., & Aburto, S. (1991). The uses and abuses of educational testing: Chicanos as a case in point. In: Valencia, R. R. (Ed.), *Chicano School Failure and Success: Research and Policy Agendas for the 1990s.* (The Stanford Series on Education and Public Policy). Basingstoke, England: Falmer Press.

Vasquez, M. J. T. (1994). Latinas. In Comas-Diaz, L. & Greene, B. (Eds.). *Women of Color: Integrating Ethnic and Gender Identities in Psychotherapy.* New York & London: Guilford Press.

Vazquez, L. A., & Garcia-Vazquez, E. (1995). Variables of success and stress with Mexican American students. *The College Student Journal*, 29(2), 221-226.

Vega, W. A., Hough, R. L., & Miranda, M. R. (1985). Modeling cross-cultural research in Hispanic mental health. In Vega, W. A., & Miranda, M. R. (Eds.), *Stress and Hispanic Mental Health: Relating to Service Delivery* (DHHS Publication No. ADM 85-1410). Washington, DC: National Institute of Mental Health.

Vigil, J. D., & Long, J. M. (1981). Unidirectional or nativist acculturation - Chicano paths to school achievement. *Human Organization*, 40, 273-277.

Wagner, B. M., & Compas, B. E. (1990). Gender, instrumentality, and expressivity: Moderators of the relation between stress and psychological symptoms during adolescence. *American Journal of Community Psychology*, 18, 383-406.

Waxman, H. C., Huang, S L., & Padron, Y. N. (1997). Motivation and learning environment differences between resilient and nonresilient Latino middle school students. *Hispanic Journal of Behavioral Sciences*, 19(2), 137-155.

Weiss, R. S. (1979). Growing up a little faster: The experience of growing up in a single-parent household. *Journal of Social Issues*, 35, 97-111.

Werner, E. E. (1989). High-risk children in young adulthood: A longitudinal study from birth to 32 years. *American Journal of Orthopsychiatry*, 59, 72-81.

Werner, E., & Smith, R. (1989). *Vulnerable but invincible: A Longitudinal Study of Resilient Children and Youth.* New York: Adams, Bannister & Cox.

Werner, E., & Smith, R. S. (1982). *Vulnerable but Invincible: A Longitudinal Study of Resilient Children and Youth.* New York: McGraw-Hill.

Wertlieb, D., Weigel, C., & Feldstein, M. (1987). Measuring children's coping. *American Journal of Orthopsychiatry*, 57, 548-560.

White, R. W. (1974). Strategies of adaptation: An attempt at systematic description. In Coelho, G. V., Hamburg, D. A., & Adams, J. E. (Eds.), *Coping and Adaptation* (pp. 47-68). New York: Basic Books.

Wills, T. A. (1986). Stress and coping in early adolescence: Relationships to substance use in urban school samples. *Health Psychology*, 5, 503-529.

Wiseman, R. (1971). Integration and attainment of immigrant secondary school students in Adelaide. *Australian Journal of Education*, 15, 253-268.

Worsham, N. L., Ey, S., & Compas, B. E. (1992). *When Mom or Dad has Cancer: II. Developmental Consistencies and Differences in Coping with Family Stress.* (submitted).

Ying, Y., Akutsu, P. D., Zhang, X., Huang, L. N. (1997). Psychological dysfunction in Southeast Asian refugees as mediated by sense of coherence. *American Journal of Community Psychology*, 25(6), 839-859.

Zea, M. C., Jarama, L., & Bianchi, F. T. (1995). Social support and psychosocial competence: Explaining the adaptation to college of ethnically diverse students. *American Journal of Community Psychology*, 23(4), 509-531

NAME AND SUBJECT INDEX

Printed in the United States
30411LVS00001B/100

9 781593 320645